Wild Turkey Harvest Management: Biology, Strategies, and Techniques

Biological Technical Publication

BTP-R5001-1999

R. Wayne Bailey, pioneering wild turkey researcher, checking successful fall turkey hunters, Pocahontas County, West Virginia, 1969.   *U.S. Forest Service, John D. Gill*

U.S. Fish & Wildlife Service

Wild Turkey Harvest Management: Biology, Strategies, and Techniques

Biological Technical Publication

BTP-R5001-1999

William M. Healy
U.S. Forest Service, Holdsworth Natural Resources Center, University of Massachusetts, Amherst MA 01003 telephone 413/545 1765

Shawn M. Powell
Department of Forestry and Wildlife Management, University of Massachusetts, Amherst, MA 01003. Present address: 660 Mountain Road, West Hartford, CT 06117
telephone 860/233 8132

The Authors

William M. Healy is a wildlife biologist with the U.S. Forest Service, Northeastern Research Station, located in Amherst, Mass. Bill has a Bachelor's degree in forestry and a Master's degree in wildlife management from Penn State University. He began his research career with the U.S. Forest Service in Morgantown, W.Va. where he studied turkey brood and winter habitat use. He earned a Ph.D. from West Virginia University studying the relationships among poult feeding activity, insect abundance, and vegetation structure. Since moving to Massachusetts in 1982 Bill has continued studies of forest wildlife habitat relationships including the effects of white-tailed deer on forest vegetation, and the relationship between acorn crops and small mammal abundance.

Shawn M. Powell earned a Bachelor's degree in ecology and evolutionary biology at the University of Rochester, New York. He completed a Master's degree in biology at the University of California, Los Angeles, studying the feeding ecology of mink and river otters inhabiting coastal Vancouver Island, British Columbia. He worked for the Environmental Resources Section at the New England Division of the U.S. Army Corps of Engineers, and later as a biologist with the U.S. Fish and Wildlife Service in Carlsbad, Calif. With the Fish and Wildlife Service he studied California gnatcatcher ecology, and worked in several other projects involving threatened or endangered songbirds, reptiles, and mammals. He returned to New England to work as a research associate for the University of Massachusetts and the Massachusetts Cooperative Fish and Wildlife Research Unit, where he studied various aspects of the ecology of fishers and black bears inhabiting western Massachusetts and southern Vermont.

Acknowledgments

This report would not have been possible without the help of all the members of the Northeast Wild Turkey Technical Committee. Under the direction of Bob Sanford, committee members had been compiling background information for two years before we started. Lively discussions about the goals and content of the project at two annual meetings provided direction to the project. Committee members generously supplied data on population status, hunting regulations, and data collection; and reviewed our efforts along the way. Special thanks go to committee members Jim Cardoza, Mike Gregonis, Gary Norman, Jim Pack, Bob Sanford, and Dave Steffen for their frequent and thoughtful discussions about various aspects of turkey biology and state regulatory procedures. John Organ, Wildlife Program Chief, Division of Federal Aid, U.S. Fish and Wildlife Service, provided the funding that made this project possible, and encouragement when we needed it most. In addition to committee members, helpful reviews were provided by Russell Alpizar, Liz Brooks, Dick Kimmel, and Steve Roberts. Special thanks go to Georgette Healy for copy editing and proofreading.

Northeast Wild Turkey Technical Committee Members:

Karen Bellamy, Ministry of Natural Resources, Ontario

Steven L. Bittner, Wildlife and Heritage Division, Maryland

Douglas Blodgett, Fish and Wildlife Department, Vermont

Philip Bozenhard, Department of Inland Fisheries and Wildlife, Maine

James E. Cardoza, Division of Fisheries and Wildlife, Massachusetts

William E. Drake, Pennsylvania Game Commission, Pennsylvania

Robert E. Eriksen, Division of Fish, Game and Wildlife, New Jersey

Michael Gregonis, Department of Environmental Protection, Connecticut

Howard Kilpatrick, Department of Environmental Protection, Connecticut

Gary W. Norman, Department of Game and Inland Fisheries, Virginia

James C. Pack, Division of Natural Resources, West Virginia

Kenneth M. Reynolds, Division of Fish and Wildlife, Delaware

Robert M. Sanford, Department of Environmental Conservation, New York

David E. Steffen, Department of Game and Inland Fisheries, Virginia

Brian C. Tefft, Division of Fish and Wildlife, Rhode Island

Theodore Walski, Fish and Game Department, New Hampshire.

This publication was funded by purchases of hunting equipment through the Federal Aid in Wildlife Restoration Program of the U.S. Fish and Wildlife Service.

Contents

Section I. Introduction

Chapter 1. Background and Goals

Wild turkey *(Meleagris gallopavo)* populations probably reached their low point in the United States in the 1930s. The invention of the cannon net in the early 1950s marked the beginning of serious restoration efforts, and by 1975 restoration efforts were in full swing in the Northeast. Since then turkeys have been restored to their ancestral range in the Northeast and beyond. Wild turkey hunting seasons are now held in all 48 continental states and the Province of Ontario, Canada. Habitat conditions improved steadily in the Northeast during the period of restoration as forests that regenerated in the early part of the century matured and farmland continued to revert to forest.

During the past 3 decades managers have emphasized restoration, and the job is now essentially complete. Research focused on learning more about the turkey's population dynamics and habitat requirements. The progress of research and restoration can be traced in the proceedings of 7 National Wild Turkey Symposia, held first in 1959 and then at 5-year intervals since 1970. Major population dynamics studies, involving hundreds of radio-tagged birds, have been completed in Iowa, Mississippi, Missouri, New York, Oregon, Virginia, West Virginia, and Wisconsin. Advances in our understanding of the species were summarized in 1992 in *The Wild Turkey, Biology and Management*, edited by James G. Dickson.

This project began in 1993 with a request from the Northeast Wildlife Administrators Association to the Northeast Wild Turkey Technical Committee "to identify the minimum set of information needed to properly manage wild turkey populations and facilitate state standardization of methods and protocols for data collection within the region." The Technical Committee is composed of the wild turkey project leaders from the northeastern United States and the Province of Ontario. The Wildlife Administrators represent state and provincial agencies with authority for managing wildlife.

At the time, 3 basic harvest strategies were in use among the 13 northeastern states (Maine to Virginia) and the Province of Ontario. Those strategies were: spring gobbler harvest only, spring gobbler harvest with limited either-sex fall harvest, and spring and fall hunting designed to maximize total harvest. There were no explicit demographic models for the various harvesting programs and there was no consensus among resource professionals about the essential data needed to evaluate the effect of harvest on wild turkey populations (Vangilder and Kurzejeski 1995:40). The

criteria used to evaluate population status and the techniques used to collect data varied among the states. Consequently, few biologists were completely comfortable with the theoretical basis for harvest management or the methods used for assessing population status.

Despite these misgivings, all state and provincial management programs were viewed as successful by biologists, administrators, and the general public. Wild turkeys had been restored across their historic range in eastern North America, hunting opportunities were increasing, populations continued to grow and expand their range while experiencing either a spring harvest or a combination of spring and fall harvest. Harvest management was based on conservative regulations and a thorough understanding of the species' life history.

Our objective is to synthesize what is known about the effects of hunting on wild turkey populations, and provide models for regulating harvest that provide ample hunting opportunity with minimal risk of overharvest. In Section II we review the biology of the species because we believe harvest management must be based on a thorough understanding of population dynamics. The chapters on life history and population dynamics describe the critical relationships among life history, population characteristics, and harvest. These chapters provide the ecological basis for harvest management.

In Section III we review the 3 basic strategies for harvesting wild turkeys. We review the assumptions on which each strategy is based and recommend procedures for regulating harvest under each strategy. The procedures we propose are straightforward and based on existing methods used in various states. The procedures are based on biology, use explicit decision variables, require collection of data at regular intervals, and specify periodic review of progress.

In Section IV we describe the techniques that are most useful for obtaining data used to regulate harvest. An enormous number of techniques has been used to study wild turkeys, and the list of techniques we reviewed is contained in Appendix C. Most of those techniques are useful research tools, but we limited this review to those that are most useful for collecting data used for harvest management.

Our basic premise is that harvest strategies must be based on population dynamics, but regulation of harvest does not require detailed measurement of demographic parameters. We believe that sound management decisions can be made from harvest data and indices of relative abundance, provided harvest goals and remedial actions to be taken when goals are not met are specified in advance, and data are reviewed periodically. The discussions of the 3 basic harvest strategies and the assumptions underpinning them will be useful to all states, because every state permitting turkey hunting uses one of these strategies. The material presented provides the ecological basis for harvesting programs, and can be used to explain the goals and reasoning behind turkey hunting regulations to the public.

In contrast, the procedures that we recommend for implementing harvest strategies should be viewed as models to be used as the need arises. The regulatory procedures provide varying degrees of protection for the turkey population. The choice of harvest strategy and regulatory procedure depends on program goals, the demand for hunting opportunities, the perceived risk of overharvesting the population, and hunter safety and satisfaction. The adage "don't fix it if it ain't broke" applies to regulating turkey harvest.

In general, risk of overharvest can be reduced by increasing control over harvest rates, and the greatest control over harvest rate is achieved by regulating hunter numbers. Strong control over harvest is not always necessary or desirable. For example, hunters in Connecticut enjoy liberal fall seasons: a 2-week firearms season and about 11 weeks of bow hunting. Hunter numbers are not regulated in either fall season. In 1997 the total fall firearms harvest was about 140 turkeys—insignificant from a population standpoint. Because the demand for the resource is low, further regulation is unnecessary.

A review of hunting programs and harvest strategies is timely. Substantial progress has been made in understanding wild turkey ecology and population dynamics. Turkey hunting continues to grow in popularity despite a decline in the rate of hunting participation among the general population. Recent trends in expanding turkey populations and improving habitat quality cannot go on indefinitely. Habitat conditions are likely to stabilize and decline as mature timber is harvested, development continues, and northeastern dairy farms and pastures disappear. As turkey populations respond to these landscape changes, turkey hunters and others will likely question harvesting programs with increasing frequency. Wildlife managers need to be able to clearly explain the biological basis for hunting, the mechanisms for regulating harvest, and the effect of harvest on populations. We view this report as a first step in providing managers with the information needed to regulate harvest. We hope this report will encourage the development of explicit harvest goals, models, and decision rules. We also hope to stimulate the development of more effective and efficient methods for monitoring harvest and estimating population abundance.

Section II. Biology

Chapter 2. Life History

This brief review provides the natural history background needed to follow the chapters on Population Dynamics and Harvest Strategies. We emphasize life history attributes that provide the basis for harvest programs. Comprehensive reviews of the species' natural history can be found in the works by Schorger (1966), Hewitt (1967a), and Dickson (1992).

The wild turkey is a large-bodied bird with striking plumage and spectacular visual and auditory displays. Average weights for adult females range from 8 to11 pounds, and for adult males from 17 to 21 pounds, but individuals can be substantially heavier (Pelham and Dickson 1992). Audubon (1967:42) noted "the great size and beauty of the wild turkey," and "its value as a delicate and highly prized article of food." Archaeological evidence indicates that Native Americans used turkeys extensively for food, so some form of harvesting has occurred for several thousand years (Aldrich 1967:6).

Wild turkeys exhibit a moderate potential for population growth. Reproduction is seasonal and the population is composed of distinct age classes. Turkeys may survive for as long as 15 years in the wild (Cardoza 1995), so theoretically there could be as many as 15 age classes. The age structure of the population serves as the basis for most population analysis and modeling efforts. Mathematical models usually simplify the age structure into 2 to 4 age classes, such as poults (0-28 days), juveniles (29 days-9 months), yearlings (10-21 months), and adults (>21 months) (Vangilder and Kurzejeski 1995, Roberts and Porter 1996).

The mating system is polygamous; males play no role in rearing young. A variable percentage of 1-year-old males is reproductively active; all males ≥ 2 years old can breed. Females are capable of reproducing at 1 year of age, but adult hens are usually more successful at hatching nests than are yearlings (Vangilder 1992:146). The polygamous mating system and age structure of the population provide the basis for a spring harvest strategy that removes primarily adult males after most hens have been mated.

Mortality rates are greatest and most variable during the early stages of life. Both eggs and poults suffer substantial losses to predators. The proportion of poults dying during the first 4 weeks after hatching generally ranges from 53% to 76%, but may be greater in some years (Vangilder 1992:151). In comparison, adult mortality rates are moderate. Mean annual survival rates of hens and gobblers, based on radio telemetry studies, have ranged from 54% to 62%. In harvested populations, hunting can account for a significant part of the annual mortality.

Wild turkey populations are characterized by annual fluctuations that may approach ±50% of the long-term mean (Mosby 1967:115-117). In northern populations, where snow cover influences food availability, winter mortality may cause short-term fluctuations by reducing the breeding population (Wunz and Hayden 1975, Porter et al. 1983). Annual fluctuations, however, are most strongly related to variation in hen nesting success and poult survival, which determine the number of young joining the population each autumn (Roberts and Porter 1996).

Nesting success and poult survival are influenced primarily by predation and weather conditions. The relationships among these variables are complex, incompletely understood, and involve direct and indirect effects of weather and interactions between weather and predation (Roberts and Porter 1998a). In south Texas, the annual productivity of Rio Grande turkeys (*M.g. intermedia*) is strongly influenced by rainfall. The timing and abundance of vegetative growth in spring depends on the amount of rain received the previous autumn, because fall rains recharge soil moisture and most spring rainfall is lost to evaporation. In dry years, vegetative growth is minimal; there is little cover for nests or food for hens and poults. Under these conditions, predation on nests and poults is increased and hen nesting effort is reduced (Beasom 1970, 1973). There may also be a relationship between weather and predation in humid eastern forests where nesting cover is generally abundant. An analysis of nest survival during incubation in southcentral New York found that nest survival was greatest during cool, dry periods and poorest during warm, wet periods. Warm, moist conditions may enhance the ability of predators to use olfactory cues to locate nests (Roberts and Porter 1998a).

Most poult mortality occurs within the first 2 weeks after hatching (Hubbard et al. 1999), and predators are responsible for most losses (Paisley et al. 1998). Weather conditions also affect poult survival, and cold, wet weather is generally associated with lower poult survival (Rolley et al. 1998). Predicting the effect of weather on reproduction is difficult because the effects of temperature and precipitation vary with poult age (Healy and Nenno 1985, Roberts and Porter 1998b). Direct loss of poults to exposure seems to be associated with extreme conditions, such as flooding or prolonged cold rain (Healy and Nenno 1985). Cold, wet weather also affects poults indirectly by reducing the availability of invertebrate foods upon which poults depend during the first weeks of life. In southcentral New York, poult survival to 2 weeks of age was negatively associated with cold temperatures during the first week and precipitation during the second week (Roberts and Porter 1998b). In general, the more temperature and precipitation deviated from the long-term average, either above or below, the greater the reduction in productivity (Bailey and Rinell 1968:32). Years of better-than-average reproduction are characterized by higher rates of nest success, poult survival, and renesting by hens. Years of poor reproduction are characterized by low rates of nest success and renesting. These annual population fluctuations need to be considered when regulating fall harvest.

In populations of most species, birth rates decline as population size increases, so maximum population growth rates occur at low population density. This phenomenon, called density-dependent population growth, is important for harvest management because classic population theory and most game and fish harvesting models are based on density-dependent growth (McCullough 1979, Getz and Haight 1989). Density-dependent population growth has not been convincingly demonstrated in wild turkeys. Behaviors or feedback mechanisms that might limit the rate of increase as turkey populations grow from low to high numbers have yet to be identified, although interference between nesting hens is a potential limiting mechanism (W.M.H. personal observation, Weinstein et al. 1996). Recent radio-telemetry studies have shown no change in recruitment rate as population density changed (Vangilder and Kurzejeski 1995). In contrast, analysis of harvest data from New York suggested that maximum population growth occurs at low population densities (Porter et al. 1990a).

Numerous observations of rapid growth in newly introduced populations also suggest that turkey populations may exhibit density-dependent growth. Because the evidence for density-dependent growth is ambiguous, most turkey population models assume a constant growth rate regardless of population size. The absence of a clear density-dependent population response in turkeys also suggests that turkeys may be more vulnerable to overharvest than species that exhibit density-dependent growth because increased growth rates will not compensate for increased harvest rates.

Mean population density varies among landscape types, such as farmland with scattered woodlots, extensive forest, or farmland-forest mosaic. We do not know the ecological carrying capacity of most landscapes for wild turkeys because both the habitat and turkey populations have been changing in recent decades as eastern forests matured and turkeys expanded into new ranges. In predominantly forested landscapes, the resources available to turkeys, and hence carrying capacity, vary annually because of the turkey's dependence on acorns and other tree seed crops. In forested landscapes, mast crops influence turkey movements during fall and winter, and some evidence suggests that fall harvest increases in years of poor mast production because flocks are more vulnerable to hunting when concentrated around alternate food sources (Menzel 1975, Wunz 1986, Pack 1994). Birds in agricultural areas are less affected by changes in natural foods because of available waste grains. In some mixed forest-agricultural areas, mast crops can still have a significant effect on movements and habitat use, especially during winter (Kurzejeski and Lewis 1990). Annual fluctuations in population size and an absence of knowledge about population response to habitat conditions require a conservative approach to fall harvest management.

Chapter 3. Population Dynamics and Models

"Understanding the dynamics of wild turkey populations and the role of harvest are critical factors in the development of a harvest management program" (Vangilder and Kurzejeski 1995:40). This statement sums up the importance of population dynamics studies, both through field studies to estimate population parameters, and through modeling studies aimed at simulating population changes based on estimated or actual population parameters. Population dynamics has been defined as changes in the size of a group of animals inhabiting a specific area (Vangilder 1992). In wild turkeys and other animals, population dynamics is determined by 3 broad processes: birth (reproduction), death (mortality, or conversely, survival), and movement (immigration and emigration) (Vangilder 1992). These 3 broad processes are affected by a number of more specific factors. Some factors are easily measurable and can be used to construct turkey population models. Other factors are difficult to quantify and can be thought of as background factors that contribute to the apparently random element of population dynamics (Fig. 3.1). Of the 3 broad processes, movement has been largely ignored in studies of turkey population dynamics, because of the difficulty in defining and monitoring a closed population of study animals. Turkey population models therefore usually assume a closed population and focus on quantifying reproductive and mortality parameters.

The following review of factors influencing the population dynamics of the wild turkey is based on studies conducted on *Meleagris gallopavo* subspecies throughout the United States, although most information exists for the eastern subspecies (*M. g. silvestris*). We attempt to summarize data for the species as a whole, and provide specific results for the eastern subspecies.

Turkey Population Models

Vangilder (1992:159) offers the following description of a population model:

> A population model is a way of mathematically combining survival- and reproductive-rate estimates to produce projections of population size and age structure through time. For a specific combination of survival and reproductive rates, a model may tell you whether a wild turkey population will grow, decline, or remain stable. A model may be useful in determining the effects of varying death rates (e.g., harvest mortality) on population size and age structure. A model

may also be useful in pointing out deficiencies in data on certain parameters or in our understanding of how population parameters are interrelated.

Given the initial population size and the sex and age structure (top of Fig. 3.1), and accurate values for several reproductive and mortality parameters (terms shown in rectangles in Fig. 3.1), it is possible to predict or project the dynamics of a given turkey population over time (Vangilder 1992). Accurate values are often difficult to obtain, so models usually project a range of possible outcomes given the best available population data.

Types of Population Models

The various types of models used to project wild turkey population dynamics, and the different levels of classifying such models, were thoroughly discussed by Porter et al. (1990b). The first distinction they made was between detailed mechanistic models that encompass many specific life history attributes, and general models that use only a few parameters. Detailed models can be useful in identifying specific attributes of a species' natural history that contribute to its population dynamics, but they require comprehensive data that may be difficult, time-consuming, and expensive to collect. Another disadvantage of detailed mechanistic models is that the combined statistical variance of many variables, when assembled into a large model, may become unacceptably large.

Porter et al. (1990b) argue that general models are often more useful than mechanistic models, particularly when the goal is projecting population growth. It is difficult, however, to determine what simple estimates of survival and reproductive rates (which may be used in more general models) mean in terms of population dynamics, because survival and reproductive rates are usually both age-specific and time-specific (Vangilder 1992:158). Suchy et al. (1990) found that models of intermediate complexity provided the best fit to actual population data.

Models may also be classified as deterministic or stochastic. A deterministic model produces one unique and repeatable prediction for a given set of parameters. In contrast, stochastic models may more realistically incorporate the natural random variation inherent in these turkey population variables. Stochastic models may be preferred for management purposes when "uncertainty in prediction is a primary concern" (Porter et al. 1990b).

Studies Utilizing Turkey Population Models

There have been few efforts aimed at modeling wild turkey populations (Suchy et al. 1990) due in part to a lack of data, particularly for mechanistic models (Vangilder and Kurzejeski 1995). Opinions differ among resource professionals about the essential data needed to either manage or model wild turkey populations, and about the necessary level of model complexity (Porter et al. 1990b). The following is a synopsis of the main turkey modeling studies conducted to date. The population parameters used or discussed in each of these studies are indicated in Fig. 3.1, and are discussed later in further detail.

The hypotheses of *additive and compensatory* mortality need to be considered before discussing specific models because the choice of hypothesis has a profound effect on model results (Suchy et al. 1983, Nichols et al. 1984, Vangilder 1992). Under the compensatory mortality hypothesis, mortality from hunting simply replaces natural mortality, and is compensated for by a decrease in natural mortality after the hunting season. Under the opposing hypothesis, hunting mortality is additive to natural mortality. There is also an intermediate hypothesis, that hunting mortality is compensatory until a threshold is reached, after which it becomes additive to natural mortality. It is important to investigate which of the 3 hypotheses appears to fit the observed cause-specific mortality data most closely. Spring hunting mortality of gobblers has usually been assumed to be additive to non-hunting mortality because natural mortality rates of gobblers are low and allow little room for compensatory mortality processes (Vangilder 1992). Fall hunting mortality appeared to be additive to natural mortality in populations in Iowa (Little et al.1990) and Wisconsin (Rolley et al. 1998). Vangilder's (1992) review of the literature found little evidence that hunting mortality was compensatory for natural mortality in turkey populations.

Lobdell et al. (1972) developed a stochastic model "to analyze the long-term effect of the addition of a spring gobbler hunt on the dynamics of a hypothetical population of eastern wild turkeys." This relatively simple model made use of, among other parameters, the immature:adult female ratio, which they assumed to be the best indicator of annual production. They used this ratio to simplify the model by taking the place of several more difficult-to-measure parameters that were used in more mechanistic turkey population models. They also assumed, and presented some evidence to support, that hunting mortality was compensatory for a simulated fall-only hunting. However, they assumed that spring hunting of gobblers was additive to the total annual mortality rate.

Suchy et al. (1983) used a deterministic model (TURKEY) to simulate autumn harvest in Iowa. They simulated both the additive and compensatory hypotheses, and found that the allowable fall hunting mortality rates were higher under the threshold hypothesis than under the additive hypothesis (9.5% vs. 4.7% for females, and 28.4% vs. 16.7% for males). They concluded that a conservative management approach, assuming that wild turkey mortality due to hunting is additive to natural mortality, is preferable. Later, Suchy et al. (1990) used a modified version of the TURKEY model (TURK4) to evaluate its ability "to project wild turkey numbers by determining if projections were correlated with winter counts of turkeys" in Iowa. Another model was used to simulate the dynamics of a Missouri wild turkey population (Vangilder and Kulowiec 1988, Vangilder 1992, Vangilder and Kurzejeski 1995). This model was both deterministic and stochastic, and assumed that hunting mortality is additive.

Finally, Roberts et al. (1995) used a deterministic model to conduct sensitivity analyses to "determine the relative importance of demographic parameters to annual population change." They also discussed the distinction between realized and potential rates (Krebs 1985:167) for nesting rates, renesting rates, and hen success (Fig. 3.1). The difference is that realized rates included mortalities, whereas potential rates excluded mortalities (Roberts et al. 1995). This dichotomy raises the point that parameters used in population models have been defined in different ways, so the results from different studies are not always directly comparable unless they are recalculated using a common methodology.

Parameters Used in Population Models

Each of the 14 parameters discussed below was used in at least one of the population models we reviewed. The relationships among parameters and population processes are diagrammed in Fig. 3.1, where parameters are shown in rectangles, and numbers within rectangles index the literature citation for the appropriate model. Turkey populations were typically partitioned into 3 age classes for modeling purposes: poults (hatch to 0.4 year old), juveniles (0.4 to 1.4 years old), and adults (≥ 1.4 years old) (Rolley et al. 1998). The terms "subadult" and "juvenile" are used interchangeably in the literature. We used these conventions for age class in the discussion of population parameters. We exclude data from studies for which age classes were combined when reviewing values that require age-specific data, unless otherwise noted.

One of the most important aspects of research on population dynamics is defining the range of parameter values (Vangilder and Kurzejeski 1995). Parameter values presented below are taken from studies summarized in Vangilder (1992), with additional data from Vangilder and Kurzejeski (1995), Roberts et al. (1995), Miller et al. (1998a,b), Paisley et al. (1998), Hubbard et al. (1999), and Keegan and Crawford (1999). Several problems arise in comparing reported parameter values. First, field methods, parameter definitions, and analyses differ among studies. Second, for many parameters, year-to-year variation is large, and generally, the longer the study the larger the range in parameter values reported. Third, there is marked regional variation in some parameter values. Regional variation is particularly evident in juvenile nesting rates and juvenile nesting success rates. Fourth, the precision of parameter estimates is influenced by sample size. Extreme values, such as 0% or 100% nest success, are often associated with small sample sizes. Finally, parameter values reflect the status of the population, with extreme values being reported for either declining or growing populations. Because of the difficulties of measuring population attributes and interpreting reported values, the initial values inserted into models are usually a combination of hard data, educated guesses, and estimates from the literature (Porter et al. 1990b).

To indicate the range in variation for individual parameters that characterize turkey populations, we report mean values and the annual extremes from each study. We give ranges of reported values for all subspecies combined, and corresponding values based only on the eastern subspecies of wild turkey.

1. Nesting rate (age-specific).
Nesting rate has been defined as the proportion of hens that attempt to nest (Vangilder 1992:145). Although the nesting rate of adult hens is generally high, that of juveniles varies among populations within a subspecies (Vangilder 1992:145-146, Miller et al. 1998b, Keegan and Crawford 1999). Considering the mean values for all years of each study, for adults this variable ranged from 72.3% (Miss.) to 100.0% (Mo., Mass., Ore.) for 13 studies on all subspecies, and from 72.3% (Miss.) to 100.0% (Mo., Mass., Ore.) for 9 studies on the eastern subspecies.

For juveniles, the mean values ranged from 7.7% (N.M.) to 100.0% (Mo., N.Y., Wis.) for 13 studies on all subspecies, and from 42.0% (Iowa) to 100.0% (Mo., N.Y.) for 9 studies on the eastern subspecies.

The extreme values (i.e., the mean of all observations for any given year) for adults ranged from 30.0% (Miss.) (based on 4 studies) to 100.0% (Iowa, Mo., Mass., Ore., N.Y., Miss., Wis.) (based on 7 studies) for all subspecies, and the same values resulted for studies on the eastern subspecies alone.

For juveniles, the extremes ranged from 0.0% (Iowa) (based on 2 studies) to 100.0% (Mo., Miss., N.Y., Wis.) (based on 5 studies). These 5 studies were all done on the eastern subspecies, and no data were presented on extremes from other subspecies.

2. Renesting rate (age-specific).
Renesting rate is defined as the proportion of hens *not* successful on their first nesting attempt that attempt to renest (Vangilder 1992:145, Vangilder and Kurzejeski 1995). In most studies, renesting rate was lower for juvenile hens than for adult hens (Vangilder 1992:145).

The means for adults ranged from 0.0% (Ore.) to 69.4%[1] (N.Y.) for 10 studies on all subspecies, and from 32.0% (Iowa) to 69.4% (N.Y.) for 7 studies on the eastern subspecies.

For juveniles, the mean values ranged from 0.0% (N.M., Ore.) to 70.0% (Minn.) for 10 studies on all subspecies, and from 12.0% (Iowa) to 70.0% (Minn.) for 7 studies on the eastern subspecies (Eastern-Merriam's subspecies for Minn.).

The extreme values for adults ranged from 0.0% (Ore., Miss.) (based on 7 studies) to 100.0% (Miss.) (based on 6 studies) for all subspecies, and from 4.0% (Ore.) (based on 5 studies) to 100.0% (Miss.) (based on 6 studies) for the eastern subspecies.

For juveniles, extremes ranged from 0.0% (Iowa, N.Y., N.M., Ore., Mo., Wis.) (based on 7 studies) to 75.0% (Mo.) (based on 5 studies) for all subspecies, and from 0.0% (Iowa, N.Y., Mo.) (based on 5 studies) to 75.0% (Mo.) (based on 5 studies) for the eastern subspecies.

3. First-nest success rate (age-specific).
First-nest success rate is the proportion of first nests from which at least 1 poult hatches (Vangilder 1992:145, Roberts et al. 1995). Considering the means for all age classes (many studies did not differentiate between juveniles and adults), this variable ranged from 7.7% (Wis., juveniles) to 62.0% (Minn., combined ages) for 8 studies on the eastern subspecies (Eastern-Merriam's subspecies for Minn.).

The extremes for all age classes ranged from 0.0% (Wis., Mo., juveniles; Miss., adults) (based on 7 studies) to 100.0% (Mo., juveniles) (based on 7 studies) for the eastern subspecies (no data presented for other subspecies).

4. Renest success rate (age-specific).
Renest success rate is the proportion of renests from which at least 1 poult hatches (Vangilder 1992:145, Roberts et al. 1995). Considering the means for all age classes (many studies did not differentiate between juveniles and adults), the mean for this variable ranged from 0.0% (Iowa, juveniles) to 72.7% (Minn., combined ages) for 8 studies on the eastern subspecies (Eastern-Merriam's subspecies for Minn.).

The extremes for all age classes ranged from 0.0% (Iowa, N.Y., Miss., Mo., Tex., Wis.) (based on 7 studies) to 100.0% (Miss., adults) (based on 6 studies) for the eastern subspecies (no data presented for other subspecies).

---

[1] Potential rate, as defined by Roberts et al. (1995).

5. Hen success rate (age-specific).
Hen success rate is the proportion of hens that are successful in hatching 1 or more live poults in the first or a subsequent nesting attempt. This rate incorporates first-nest success, renesting rate, and renest success. Hens that do not attempt to nest are not included (Vangilder 1992). For eastern wild turkeys, adult hen success rate tends to be higher than juvenile hen success rate.

The means[2] for adults ranged from 24.6% (Miss.) to 82.8% (Pa.), based on 25 studies on all subspecies. The same values result from the 16 studies on the eastern subspecies alone.

For juveniles, the means range from 0.0% (Tex.) to 100.0% (Pa.), based on 15 studies on all subspecies. For the eastern subspecies alone, the means range from 15.4% (Ala.) to 100.0% (Pa.), based on 10 studies.

The extreme values for adults ranged from 0.0% (Tex.) to 90.0% (Ga.), based on 16 studies on all subspecies. For the eastern subspecies alone, the means range from 5.0% (Miss.) to 90.0% (Ga.) based on 11 studies.

For juveniles, the extremes range from 0.0% (Mo., Iowa, Ala., Tex., Wis.), to 100.0% (Mo., Pa.) based on 9 studies on all subspecies. The same extremes result from examining 8 studies of the eastern subspecies alone.

6. Clutch size (age-specific, nesting-attempt-specific).
Clutch size is simply the number of eggs laid by a hen, whether fertile or not, for a given nesting attempt. Vangilder and Kurzejeski (1995) observed no difference in clutch size between juveniles and adults. However, no distinction was made between clutch size in juveniles versus adults in many studies, so only 1 value is reported here.

For first nests, the mean for this variable ranged from 8.5 (N.M.) to 12.7 (Mich.) for 11 studies on all subspecies, and from approximately 9 (Iowa)[3] to 12.7 (Mich.) for 8 studies on the eastern subspecies.

In most studies, clutch sizes were larger in first nests than in renests. For renests, the mean ranged from 7.0 (Iowa, juveniles)[4] to 11.9 (N.Y.) for 11 studies on all subspecies, and from 7.0 (Iowa, juveniles) to 11.9 (N.Y.) for 8 studies on the eastern subspecies.

7. Hatchability: hatching success, fecundity; age-specific, nesting-attempt-specific.
Hatchability is generally defined as the percentage of all eggs that hatch for successful nests (Vangilder 1992:149-150, Roberts et al. 1995, Vangilder and Kurzejeski 1995). Thus, as indicated in Fig. 3.1, egg fertility, embryo viability, and partial predation are all encompassed by hatching success (Vangilder 1992:149). Some seasonal differences are apparent, but hen age does not seem to have much effect on hatching success (Vangilder 1992:149). For all nesting attempts combined, the mean values for this variable range from 80.0% (Minn., Pa.) to 93.0% (N.Y.) for 15 studies on all subspecies. The same values result from the 10 studies on the eastern subspecies.

8. Poult mortality rate.
There is some evidence that poult mortality is higher for broods from juvenile hens than from adult hens (Glidden and Austin 1975). Poult mortality is greatest during the first 2 weeks post-hatching (Vangilder 1992:150), after which time poult mortality declines sharply (Vangilder and Kurzejeski 1995). It is difficult to monitor poult mortality after 4 weeks of age because hens tend to form multiple brood flocks (Suchy et al. 1990, Roberts et al. 1995, Vangilder and Kurzejeski 1995). Rolley et al. (1998) assumed that poult survival between 28 days post-hatching and 1 October equaled that of adult females. They point out, however, that not much is known about poult mortality during this phase. Furthermore, it is difficult to compare estimates of poult survival among studies because of differences in the methods used to assess poult survival (Roberts et al. 1995). To give a rough idea of the range of variation, considering the means, at 2 weeks of age mortality rate ranged from approximately 46-47% (Mo., Wis.) to 73% (Ala.) for 11 studies on all subspecies, and the same values resulted from 10 studies on the eastern subspecies only.

At 4 weeks of age, the means ranged from 40.4% (Iowa) to 76% (N.Y.) for 9 studies on all subspecies, and the same values resulted from 8 studies on the eastern subspecies only.

Considering the extreme values, at 2 weeks of age the range was from 21.1% (Iowa) to 88% (Tex.) for 4 studies on the eastern subspecies (no data presented for other subspecies). At 4 weeks of age the extremes ranged from 35% (Tex.) to 88% (Tex.) for 3 studies on the eastern subspecies (no data presented for other subspecies).

9. Juvenile and adult survival rate.
Population models require separate survival rates for each season, and for each age and sex class. Mortalities are attributed to specific causes. The largest source of mortality in most studies is predation (Vangilder 1992:155, Roberts et al. 1995, Vangilder and Kurzejeski 1995). Categorized mortality data are not generally comparable among studies because of differences in calculating mortality rates, classifying mortality factors, and defining time intervals for calculating mortality (Vangilder and Kurzejeski 1995). Examining overall annual survival rates provides a rough comparison of the variation in survival rates among different regions (Vangilder 1992:154). The following data are for various combinations of sex and age classes.

---

[2] Excluding a study in Texas (Beasom and Pattee 1980) in which the age of the hens was not specified and where it was unknown whether a hen attempted to nest unless then hen reached incubation. The mean was in this study was 17.0%
[3] Ranged from 8.8 for juveniles to 9.4 for adults.
[4] From 8.0 (Ala.), if only the 9 studies where age classes were combined are considered.

Considering means, survival rate ranges from 15% (Va., juvenile and adult gobblers, hens) to 75% (Mass., adult hens) for 15 studies on all subspecies. The same data result from 13 studies on the eastern subspecies.

Considering the extremes, this variable ranges from 7.8% (Iowa, juvenile gobblers) to 100.0% (Iowa, juvenile hens) for 4 studies on the eastern subspecies (no data for other subspecies).

10. Harvest mortality rate.
Harvest mortality rates differ between spring gobbler season and fall either-sex seasons. Adult gobblers are more vulnerable than juvenile males to spring harvest (Vangilder 1992:156-157). Fall harvest mortality rates also differ by age class and sex, with juvenile males being the most vulnerable and hens being least vulnerable to fall harvest (Little et al. 1990). Harvest rates are often calculated for combinations of age or sex classes to increase sample size.

It is usually desirable to enter a range of harvest mortality rates into a model to examine how the turkey population would respond to different management strategies. After performing such manipulations, both the Missouri model (Vangilder and Kulowiec 1988) and the Suchy et al. (1983) model predict that sustained fall harvests of <10% (for both males and females) permit continued population growth, but sustained fall harvests greater than this level predict rapid population declines (Little et al. 1990, Vangilder 1992:163). Furthermore, based on data input into these models, spring gobbler harvests of <30% will also allow continued population growth (Vangilder 1992:163).

For gobblers, during a spring hunting season, previous management regimes have reported harvest of up to 51% of the estimated population (Ala., Gardner et al. 1973). For hens, during a fall hunting season up to 89% of a radio-tagged population has been reported harvested (Fla., Williams et al. 1980).

11. Young per adult female.
This parameter has been used in simple mechanistic models to represent the number of young entering the population at some specific time. Values have been expressed as number of young per adult female (Lobdell et al. 1972) and female young recruited per female (Porter et al. 1990b). This parameter has been used when other demographic data, such as hen success rate, hatchability rate, and poult survival, were unavailable. More detailed models predict recruitment from estimates of fecundity and survival rates, and validate predictions by comparing them with observations of poults/hen or juveniles/adult in the harvest (Rolley et al. 1998).

Lobdell et al. (1972) calculated that a mean of 3.025 young per adult female (range 2.275-3.775) was needed to maintain a population of approximately 1,000 turkeys for a 100-year period. No directly comparable data were presented in other population model papers reviewed.

12. Sex ratio of poults at hatching.
There are no comparative data presented in any of the population model papers reviewed. Therefore, no among-studies range of variation is reported here. Vangilder and Kurzejeski (1995) and Suchy et al. (1983) assumed a 50:50 sex ratio for their models.

13. Sex ratio of adults.
This parameter is highly variable among studies depending in part on the time of year and the intensity of the spring gobbler hunt. For Suchy et al.'s (1983) study in Iowa, this percentage ranged from 43.1% to 64.1% female for juveniles, and from 61.6% to 74.0% female for adults. Rolley et al. (1998) initialized their model with 50% adult females and 50% adult males and generated a mean stable sex and age distribution of 33% adult females, 18% juvenile females, 30% adult males, and 18% juvenile males.

14. Starting population size: age-specific and sex-specific.
This parameter varies among studies depending on the current status of the population, and on how the population is defined. It is difficult to estimate turkey population sizes with current census techniques (Vangilder 1992:161), but it is necessary to estimate a value for this parameter to use many population models. Initial population size has been estimated in many ways, and initial values are often ad hoc estimates derived from several sources of information.

Conclusions: Evaluation of Parameters

Sensitivity analysis is an important step in the modeling process. This analysis involves systematically varying the values for each variable to determine which variable has the greatest influence on population change, and the values of each variable that produce significant population change (Porter et al. 1990b).

Sensitivity analysis by Suchy et al. (1983) suggested that variation in female survival was more important than variation in reproduction in influencing population trends. The simulations of Vangilder and Kurzejeski (1995) show that increasing nest success or decreasing poult mortality could have a large positive effect on turkey population growth. Similarly, after performing a sensitivity analysis on the variables entered into their model, Roberts et al. (1995) found that nest success was the most important and most variable parameter influencing population dynamics. Nest success was more important than poult survival or annual adult survival, but all 3 variables had a significant effect on population change. Other parameters they examined were unimportant contributors to population change. Roberts and Porter (1996) later found that variation in nest success and survival of juveniles, yearlings, and adults had similar effects on annual changes in abundance. Rolley et al. (1998) similarly placed greater importance on the influence of poult survival, and found that both reproduction and survival are important in controlling population growth. Nest success and poult survival are difficult to control through management practices (Vangilder and Kurzejeski 1995). Harvest, particularly fall either-sex harvest, is easier to control, and perhaps more important for population regulation (Vangilder and Kurzejeski 1995, Rolley et al. 1998).

Regardless of the parameter values used to model population dynamics, all parameters should be carefully defined, preferably using definitions common to other recent modeling literature. Long-term studies are necessary for defining the yearly range of variation of a given parameter for a given geographic area. In the absence of sufficient data on yearly variability for a population of interest, extreme or mean values from other areas can be used as boundaries within which a stochastic population model can be allowed to vary to test the effects of various permutations of these variables. If a sensitivity analysis can be used to identify parameters that have a large influence on population change, the model can be simplified to reduce the problems of excessive variances associated with complex models. In this manner the cost and effort of collecting data needed to predict changes in turkey populations can be minimized.

Figure 3.1. Some measurable parameters and factors known to or suspected of affecting wild turkey population dynamics.

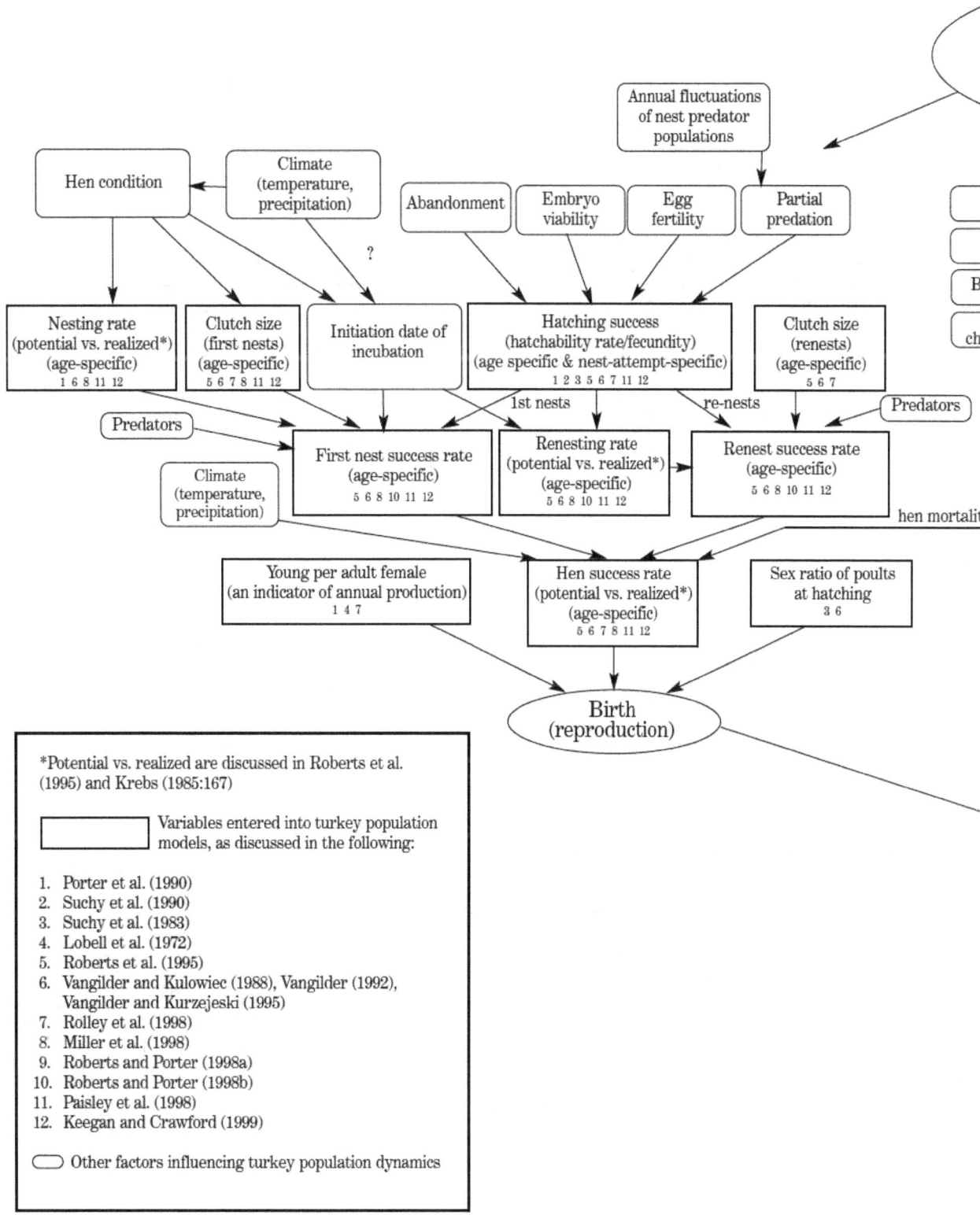

*Potential vs. realized are discussed in Roberts et al. (1995) and Krebs (1985:167)

Variables entered into turkey population models, as discussed in the following:

1. Porter et al. (1990)
2. Suchy et al. (1990)
3. Suchy et al. (1983)
4. Lobell et al. (1972)
5. Roberts et al. (1995)
6. Vangilder and Kulowiec (1988), Vangilder (1992), Vangilder and Kurzejeski (1995)
7. Rolley et al. (1998)
8. Miller et al. (1998)
9. Roberts and Porter (1998a)
10. Roberts and Porter (1998b)
11. Paisley et al. (1998)
12. Keegan and Crawford (1999)

Other factors influencing turkey population dynamics

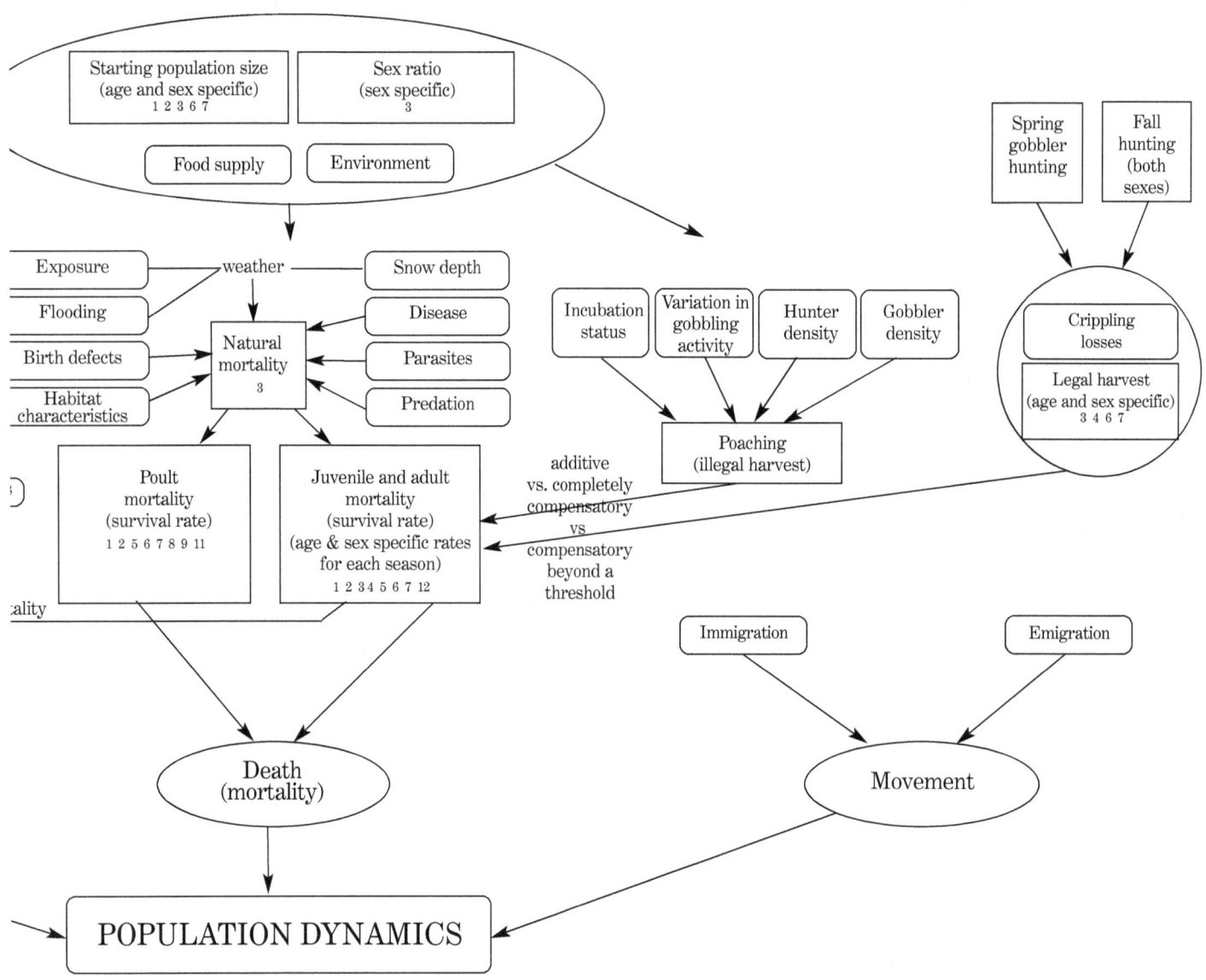

Section III. Harvesting Strategies

Three basic strategies are used to harvest wild turkeys: (1) harvest only gobblers in the spring; (2) harvest gobblers in the spring and allow limited harvest of birds of either sex in the fall; and (3) attempt to maximize the combined spring gobbler and fall either-sex harvests. It might seem that many harvest strategies could be developed, but given the species' life history and North American hunting traditions we believe these 3 strategies are the only practical options for turkey harvest management.

Spring gobbler hunting is biologically the most conservative approach. This strategy yields stable harvests and is unlikely to result in overharvest. In contrast, experience has shown that fall harvest can depress population growth. Population studies and models have shown that turkey populations are particularly sensitive to adult hen mortality. Removals of more than 10% of the population during fall season are likely to lead to population decline (Suchy et al. 1983, Vangilder and Kurzejeski 1995). Vulnerability of adult hens to fall harvest is influenced by poult recruitment because juveniles are more susceptible to harvest than adults. When reproduction is poor there are few juveniles in the population to buffer the effect of fall hunting on adults. Mast crops may also affect fall harvest. In Pennsylvania and West Virginia some of the largest fall harvests occurred during the years of poor mast production. Strategies that include fall harvest are inherently more complex than the strategy of harvesting gobblers in the spring because all age and sex classes are harvested, managers must deal with annual variation in population size, and under some conditions food resources affect vulnerability to hunting.

The strategy of maximizing the combined spring and fall harvest is analogous to the maximum sustained yield strategies used for white-tailed deer and fish populations. Turkey harvest strategy, however, differs in important ways. First, turkey harvest occurs twice during the year and each harvest removes different segments of the population. Second, maximum sustained yield strategies for other species assume a stable carrying capacity and density-dependent population responses that cause the population to oscillate around carrying capacity. In contrast, we assume that wild turkey populations are density independent and subject to short-term fluctuations that are related to annual variation in recruitment. Another complication arises in some northeastern habitats where vulnerability to fall harvest may increase when mast crops fail. Both turkey recruitment and mast crops are correlated with weather variables, but, as yet, neither can be predicted from weather data. Furthermore, neither recruitment nor mast production have regular cycles that can be used to predict future conditions. Therefore, fall turkey populations are moving targets. Optimizing fall harvest requires a measure of turkey abundance prior to hunting and the ability to regulate hunting effort. In this section we will start with spring gobbler harvest and end with optimizing the combined spring and fall harvest.

Chapter 4. Spring Gobblers-Only Harvest

Spring harvest strategies are designed to remove primarily adult males after most breeding has taken place. In theory, this type of harvest has minimal effect on population growth rates because mating is polygamous and males play no role in rearing young. Extensive management experience has shown the strategy of post-breeding male harvest to be ecologically sound and sustainable. Although the strategy is clear, actually regulating the harvest is complex.

The following assumptions form the core of spring harvest management in the Northeast. The assumptions are not independent. Here we review each assumption, show how it may be violated, and identify hunting regulations designed to assure the assumptions are met.

Assumption 1: Spring harvest is limited to males.
Violations of this assumption are insignificant for legal harvests. Regulations in 10 northeastern states and Ontario allow taking bearded birds. In theory, this regulation puts up to 10% of the adult hen population at risk (Schorger 1957), but in practice the legal harvest of bearded hens is rare (Vangilder 1996). In Massachusetts, over 19 years, there was an average of 1 bearded hen taken per 122 males (J.E. Cardoza, unpubl. data).

Illegal taking of hens is a potentially serious violation of this assumption. In Missouri, over 7 spring seasons, 5.2% of the hens were shot illegally (Vangilder and Kurzejeski 1995). Illegal taking of hens was also significant in Virginia and West Virginia (J.C. Pack, pers. commun.). In Missouri, Virginia, and West Virginia, the loss of hens to poaching can exceed the legal harvest of hens during fall either-sex seasons. Losses of this magnitude can have a negative effect on population growth, especially in populations also subjected to fall either-sex harvest (Suchy et al. 1983, Vangilder and Kurzejeski 1995). Population modeling suggests that removal of more than 10% of the adult hen population will reduce rates of population growth.

Illegal taking of hens is difficult to detect and manage. Regulations that establish the dates of hunting, restrict shooting hours, and prescribe hunting methods (e.g., calls must be used) are designed to minimize the loss of hens.

Assumption 2: Hunting mortality is additive to natural mortality.
Most game harvest models assume that hunting mortality partially or wholly replaces natural mortality (Caughley 1985). In the simplest model, complete compensation, harvesting does not affect the population size unless its rate exceeds some threshold value. As long as harvest remains below the threshold, a corresponding decrease in other forms of mortality will compensate for increased hunting mortality. More complex models of partial compensation assume a density-dependent population response in which rate of population growth increases as population size decreases.

For wild turkeys, a growing body of evidence indicates that hunting mortality is additive to natural mortality (J.C. Pack, unpubl. data). Wild turkey populations have generally shown a linear increase in overall mortality with increasing hunting mortality (Little et al. 1990, Vangilder and Kurzejeski 1995). Adult gobblers have high survival rates outside of hunting season, so there is little opportunity for compensating increases in survival to offset hunting mortality (Suchy et al. 1983, Little et al. 1990). As a result, turkey population models are generally based on the assumption that hunting mortality is additive to natural mortality, and we recommend this approach to harvest management.

Assumption 3: Spring harvest does not affect long-term population levels.
This assumption is widely held, and experience with the management of harvested populations suggests the assumption of no long-term effect has generally been true. Turkey populations have expanded and thrived throughout North America while being subjected to conservative spring harvests. Detailed population studies show that the rate of spring harvest can affect population dynamics and breeding behavior. This assumption would be violated if most adult males were harvested each year, or if breeding behavior were disrupted by either an inappropriately timed season or excessive harvest.

Population modeling suggests that a spring harvest of 30% of the male population would allow for continued population growth and provide quality hunting (Vangilder 1992). Precise estimates of gobbler harvest rates, either as a percentage of the gobbler population or the total population, are unavailable for spring hunting in the Northeast. Harvest rates from other eastern states, determined primarily from radio-tracking and band recovery studies, have been variable, ranging from about 15% to 51% of the gobbler population (Vangilder 1992:156-157). In southwestern Wisconsin, spring harvest removed an average of 32% of the gobbler population (Paisley et al. 1996). Long-term population studies and simulation models from Missouri illustrate the relationships between harvest rate and population characteristics (Vangilder 1992:162, Vangilder and Kurzejeski 1995:29). As harvest rates increase, the proportion of adult males in the population declines and the proportion of juveniles in the harvest increases. Harvesting more than 25% of the adult gobblers each year would shift the age structure in favor of juvenile males. A total harvest rate of 60% would remove all adult males in some years and, on average, produce a spring population consisting of only 10% adult males. Such an intensive harvest would affect both population dynamics and the quality of hunting.

Although the harvest of gobblers in the spring has been described as "practically foolproof" (Bailey and Rinell 1968:53), it is clear that this assumption depends on maintaining a reasonable rate of harvest. None of the northeastern states or provinces has expressed spring harvest goals in terms of desired harvest rate, but all agencies have established regulations to ensure a conservative harvest rate. The regulations that directly affect gobbler harvest rate include season timing, season length, bag limit, and limits on numbers of hunters. The best available evidence suggests that gobbler harvest $\leq$30% are sustainable, and that current regulations are maintaining harvest rates at sustainable levels.

Assumption 4: Spring gobbler hunting does not disrupt breeding behavior.

This assumption is an integral part of the preceding one that spring hunting does not affect population levels. Discussion of Assumption 3 emphasizes the effects of harvest rate on population demography. Assumption 4 also considers harvest rate, but focuses on the timing of the hunt relative to the chronology of reproduction and the direct and indirect effects of hunting on nesting success.

The goal of spring hunting has been to maximize hunter opportunity for taking a gobbler and minimize risk to nesting hens. One strategy for accomplishing this goal has been to start the spring hunt near the median date for the onset of incubation. Thus, hunting starts well after the onset of seasonal gobbling activity and after most breeding has taken place. In theory, incubating hens are protected by their secretive nature and the advanced stage of vegetative growth. Hunter opportunities are good because "gobbling reaches a second peak when the bulk of the hens are incubating and no longer meet with the males" (Bailey and Rinell 1967:73). Conventional wisdom held that gobblers were more vulnerable to hunters' calls early in the reproductive season, and that early seasons might lead to excessive harvest rates and a shortage of breeding males (Kurzejeski and Vangilder 1992:177). This effect was reported from southern Alabama, where intensive hunting apparently caused a shortage of breeding males resulting in a significant proportion of infertile clutches and lowered overall productivity (Exum et al. 1987:43-44).

The effect of the timing of spring season on the rate of illegal killing of hens has not been measured. There is some evidence that incubating hens are less vulnerable to poaching than non-reproductive hens (Miller 1997). In Missouri, more hens were lost to poaching in years when spring gobbler season began before peak incubation (Vangilder 1992:155). In Virginia and West Virginia, illegal kill was also greater when gobbler season began before the peak of incubation, and survival rates of nesting hens were always greater than those of non-nesting hens (J.C. Pack, unpubl. data). Reported rates of poaching vary regionally, and the rates are not necessarily greater where spring seasons start earlier and last longer (e.g., Miller 1997). Because poaching is believed to be a potential problem, most eastern states cite protection of hens as another reason for holding spring seasons while the bulk of the hens are incubating. In contrast to poaching, legal spring hunting clearly has minimal effect on hen nesting success.

Hunting Regulations

Regulations affecting spring gobbler season in the Northeast are summarized in Table 4.1. In this section, we describe the relationship of each regulation to the assumptions underpinning spring harvest strategies, and we examine the effect of each regulation on harvest rate.

Table 4.1. Summary of spring gobbler season regulations in use in the Northeast in 1996.

Regulation	CT	DE	ME	MD	MA	NH	NJ	NY	ONT	PA	RI	VT	VA	WV
Season length, weeks														
3	x	x							x					
4+			x	x	x	x	x	x		x	x	x	x	x
Bag limit														
1	x	x	x			x			x	x	x			
2	x			x	x	x	x	x				x	x	x
Bearded birds	x	x	x	x	x			x	x	x		x	x	x
Males						x	x				x			
Regulate hunter numbers														
None				x		x		x	x	x		x	x	x
Number	x	x	x		x		x				x			
Area														
Time		x												
Time and area	x						x							
Method of taking														
Calling only							x				x			
Unspecified	x	x	x	x	x	x		x	x	x		x	x	x
Hunting implement														
Shotgun & shot size	x	x	x	x	x	x	x	x	x	x	x	x		
Archery gear	x	x		x	x	x	x		x	x	x			
Muzzle-loading shotgun		x			x			x		x		x		
Shotgun, rifle, bow													x	x
Harvest reporting														
Check station	x	x	x	x	x	x	x		x		x	x	x	x
Report card	x	x						x		x	x			

Season Dates and Season Length

Proper timing of the spring gobbler season is considered critical for protecting the population. The dates and length of the spring hunting season affect Assumptions 1, 3, and 4 about spring harvest. The biological gobbling season spans the entire reproductive cycle. Gobbling activity begins in late winter before breeding takes place and gradually ends about 3 months later when nests begin to hatch. Thus, the later a hunting season starts in the reproductive cycle the closer it is to the end of gobbling activity and the shorter it must be.

The northeastern states and provinces generally have seasons that coincide with the incubation period rather than the full gobbling season. Thus, in the Northeast most seasons are 3 or 4 weeks long, starting in late April or early May and running through May. Starting the hunting season near the onset of incubation serves 2 goals: providing hunters ample opportunity to hear gobblers and protecting hens from inadvertent kill (Miller et al. 1997). Recent studies have reported a single peak in gobbling that did not coincide with the start of incubation (Kienzler et al. 1996, Miller et al. 1997). In West Virginia, the number of gobblers heard per hour declines steadily over the season, which starts on the fourth Monday of April and lasts 4 weeks (Igo et al. 1997). That pattern of gobbling activity seems typical for populations in the Northeast.

Incubation behavior does appear to provide hens some protection from poaching. West Virginia gobbler hunters reported seeing and calling-in most hens during the first week of the season, and the numbers declined steadily as the season progressed (Igo et al. 1997: Table 10, p. 15). Human attitudes, however, may affect poaching rates more than the dates of the hunting season. Illegal taking of hens during spring gobbler season is significant in Virginia and West Virginia (G. Norman, J.C. Pack, pers. commun.), and in some years in Missouri (Vangilder and Kurzejeski 1995), but not in Mississippi (Miller 1997). Strong regional variation obscures the relationships among hen mortality and the dates and length of spring hunting season.

The following generalizations can be made about the affects of hunting season timing and length on harvest.

■ Starting seasons early in the reproduction cycle will maximize hunter opportunity to hear and harvest gobblers (Miller 1997). Early, intensive harvest may affect population dynamics (Assumption 3) and breeding behavior (Assumption 4) (Exum et al. 1987). Risk of overharvest can be minimized in early seasons by using a permit system to regulate hunter density.

■ Shortening the spring season will reduce rates of gobbler harvest. The reduction in harvest will be greatest when a shortened season occurs late in the reproductive cycle (Kurzejeski and Vangilder 1992:177).

■ At present, we cannot predict the size of the reduction in harvest that will be accomplished by incrementally shortening or delaying spring hunting season. Managers should recognize that season length and timing provide only weak control over harvest rate. Strong control over harvest rate requires regulating hunter density.

■ Strong regional variation obscures the relationship between season timing and illegal taking of hens. It is clear, however, that the timing of spring season has the potential to reduce illegal killing of hens, and experience in several eastern states recommends the conservative approach of having spring seasons coincide with peak incubation. Regional variation in poaching activity also suggests that hunter training and law enforcement may be appropriate tools for reducing hen mortality during spring season.

Bag Limits
Bag limits are pertinent to all 4 assumptions about spring gobblers harvest. Bag limits are either 1 or 2 birds in the Northeast. Ontario and 5 states have a 1-bird limit, 7 other states allow taking 2 birds, and Connecticut has a 1-bird limit on public land and a 2-bird limit on private land. Bag limits restrict the activities of the most efficient hunters, distribute the harvest among hunters, and set an upper limit on the harvest. Increasing bag limits can increase hunting opportunity. In practice, raising the limit from 1 to 2

birds has had little effect on total harvest. In West Virginia, a total of 22,741 gobblers were reported harvested during the 1997 and 1998 spring seasons, and 7.5% of the hunters reported killing 2 birds (J.C. Pack, unpub. data). Bag limits provide only weak control over harvest rate, because only states with multiple bird limits have the option to reduce harvest by restricting bag limit. When conditions permit, increasing bag limits can increase hunting opportunity with little risk to the population.

Only New Hampshire, New Jersey, and Rhode Island specify that spring hunting is limited to males; 10 other states and Ontario allow taking bearded birds. Legal harvest of bearded hens is insignificant.

Control of Hunter Numbers
Hunter numbers and hunter effort affect harvest rate (Assumption 3) and breeding behavior (Assumption 4). Ontario and 7 northeastern states do not regulate hunter numbers. In some of these states hunters are required to have a special permit or license, but all applicants receive a permit. Connecticut, Delaware, New Jersey, Rhode Island, and Maine, use a lottery or random drawing system to restrict hunter numbers. In Connecticut and New Jersey applicants must choose a season specific to an area and time period.

Regulation of hunter numbers by zone or turkey management unit provides strong control over harvest. Permit allocations can be adjusted annually in response to changes in the turkey population or other factors within the management zone. The permit system allows managers to identify the hunting population and obtain additional information as needed.

Methods of Taking
New Jersey and Connecticut specify the method of taking as "calling" and prohibit "stalking." This restriction is intended to protect hens from inadvertent kill (Assumption 1) and enhance safety. None of the other states explicitly state a method of taking, but many states prohibit the use of bait, electronic calls, and dogs. The effectiveness of these regulations is unknown.

Hunting Hours
Hunting hours are from 30 minutes before sunrise until noon or 1:00 pm. These hours are intended to protect nesting hens (Assumption 1), because incubating hens are believed to leave the nest to feed in the afternoon. The effect of this regulation on hen mortality is unknown.

Hunting Implement
Restrictions on hunting implements are intended to promote hunting safety. Virginia and West Virginia have no limits on hunting implement, but Ontario and other northeastern states restrict hunters to the use of shotguns and specific shot sizes. Delaware, Massachusetts, New York, and Ontario allow muzzle-loading shotguns in addition to modern shotguns. Nine states also allow hunters to use bows.

Harvest Reporting

An accurate measure of harvest is considered critical for harvest management programs. In the Northeast, reporting of kill is universal and generally mandatory. The majority of states and Ontario require successful hunters to bring birds to check stations. Maine and Rhode Island also require hunters to return a kill report form by mail. Connecticut requires fall firearms hunters to present birds at a check station; spring gobbler and fall archery hunters use kill report forms. Pennsylvania and New York do not operate check stations and require hunters to return a kill report form, although in New York reporting is not legally mandatory. Compliance with reporting requirements varies among states, and over time within states. All states consider non-reporting a serious source of error in harvest estimates and formally evaluate reporting rates with post-season mail or phone surveys.

Decision Variables and Regulatory Procedures

Agencies in the Northeast generally express turkey management goals in qualitative rather than quantitative terms. The most common goals include re-establishing viable populations in all suitable habitat and allowing sustained harvest without adverse impact on the resource. Other commonly expressed goals include maintaining populations in balance with available habitat and other resources, and sustaining populations for esthetic, scientific, and educational values. Agencies seldom express harvest goals in terms of harvest density (kill/unit area), harvest rate (percent of population), or population density. The West Virginia Division of Natural Resources has a harvest goal of a minimum of 1 gobbler/mile^2 of range. Minnesota has a harvest goal of 30% of the gobbler population (Appendix A).

Regulations used to achieve these goals fall into 2 categories: those designed to protect the resource and those addressing hunting quality and safety. Some agencies regulate hunter numbers and others do not. Controls on hunter numbers are used primarily to protect the population, but limiting hunter participation directly affects hunting quality by establishing a maximum hunter density. Hunter numbers generally are controlled through a system of random drawings for a limited number of permits (Connecticut, Delaware, Maine, New Jersey, Rhode Island). Hunters must choose a hunting unit, time period, or a combination of the two. Limited permit systems provide a mechanism for distributing the harvest among hunters and management units. States that do not limit hunter numbers may require a turkey hunting permit, but permits are available to all applicants, and generally hunters may hunt when and where they want within the region open to hunting. Both management approaches–limited and unrestricted hunter numbers–use harvest trend data to monitor population response and are based on the same assumptions. The strategy of unrestricted hunter numbers allows only coarse control over harvest rate. Permit systems that limit hunter numbers allow adjusting harvest annually in response to harvest and population trends and provide much finer control over harvest rate.

Spring Gobbler Harvest, No Control on Hunter Numbers

This approach represents the simplest harvest management model in terms of regulatory structure and information needs. The turkey population is protected by the regulation of season timing, season length, and bag limit. Hunt quality and safety are addressed by regulations that specify hunting methods (calls must be used; no stalking), hunting implement (shotgun, shot size restrictions), hunting hours, and blaze orange. In addition, hunt quality, hunter ethics, and safety are maintained through hunter education and a variety of continuing education and out-reach activities. These efforts also serve to protect the population by encouraging behaviors that limit the harvest to males (Assumption 1).

Harvest trends are used to monitor population status. Declining harvests may trigger more restrictive regulations (e.g., later, shorter seasons) and increasing harvest may lead to more liberal harvest (increase bag limit). Accurate measure of harvest represents the basic information need, and harvest is assumed to provide a reliable index to population size (Lint et al.1995).

This harvest strategy is simple and has been successful. Many eastern states began their modern turkey hunting seasons with restrictions on hunter numbers and then relaxed controls when trends in hunter numbers and harvest suggested controls were unnecessary. The beauty of this system is in its regulatory simplicity. Usually, there is 1 statewide season and license or permit holders can hunt when and where they want. Harvest is measured with mandatory check stations, mail-back report cards, or a combination of the two. The system regulates state-wide harvest. This strategy cannot address local problems of under- or over-harvest and it cannot distribute hunters to reduce interference among hunters and improve hunting quality. Safety can be a concern when accident rates increase (e.g., Pa. and Mo.).

Permit systems facilitate identifying the turkey hunting segment of the general hunting population for delivering safety messages or obtaining additional information. Permit systems allow random sampling of turkey hunters to estimate harvest, effort, reporting compliance rates, and other attributes.

We recommend the following procedures for regulating spring gobbler harvest where hunter numbers are uncontrolled.

1. Stratify the overall area into Turkey Management Units (TMUs).
Options:
a. ecologically based units, e.g., physiographic regions.

b. political units, e.g., counties, townships.
c. combination of ecological and political units, e.g., aggregate counties to approximate physiographic units.

2. Establish a long-term minimum harvest goal for each TMU, and specify remedial actions to be taken if harvest falls below the goal.

For example, if harvest falls below goal for 2 consecutive years, season opening will be delayed by 1 week and the season will be shortened by 1 week.

Note that when hunter numbers are unregulated, the controls over harvest rate are limited to season timing, season length, and bag limit. An alternative response to declining harvests is to institute a permit system that limits hunter numbers. An existing TMU system provides the basis for a permit system and a minimum harvest goal provides a decision rule for protecting the population before it experiences a serious decline. Therefore, we recommend that TMUs and minimum harvest goals be established as safeguards.

3. Measure harvest annually by TMU.
Options include one or more of the following:
a. mandatory check stations.
b. mandatory kill report card.
c. post-season surveys of hunters.
Harvest data are a critical information need. Post-season surveys are often used to check on reporting rates obtained with check stations or report cards.

4. Monitor hunter effort as expressed by numbers of hunters and trips or hours per hunter.
Options include:
a. post-season surveys.
b. mail-back questionnaires with permit.
Hunter effort data provide a check on the validity of harvest as an index to population size. Effort data needs to include unsuccessful hunters so a permit system facilitates gathering these data.

5. Obtain an annual index to population size that is independent of harvest.
Options include:
a. random surveys of hunters pursuing other species. For example, Minnesota conducts a random survey of antlerless deer permit holders to derive indices of turkey abundance and data on the distribution of turkeys (Welsh and Kimmel 1990, Kimmel et al. 1996).
b. volunteer-cooperator reports.
For example, West Virginia uses a volunteer deer bow hunter survey to obtain data on the abundance and distribution of many species (Glassock et al. 1997).
c. staff/volunteer sighting records.
For example, summer brood sighting records maintained by Pennsylvania Game Commission field officers (Wunz and Shope 1980, Wunz and Ross 1990).

An independent index to population is not critical to the decision process with this strategy. However, we recommend obtaining a second index to abundance as a check on harvest trend data. Should the

management agency decide to restrict harvest by limiting hunter numbers an independent index to abundance is particularly useful for establishing permit quotas.

Spring Gobbler Harvest, Hunter Numbers Regulated
Regulating hunter numbers through a permit system allows much finer control over harvest than the preceding approach. Permit systems generally have been used to protect the population, but they have also been used to satisfy hunter demand for a "quality" low hunter-density experience. Hunter numbers can be controlled by TMU and hunting season segment. The number of permits can be adjusted annually in response to harvest trends and other available information on population trends and hunter satisfaction. Issues of hunt quality that relate to crowding and interference among hunters can be addressed directly.

A good example of the degree of control that can be achieved by regulating hunter numbers is provided by the model developed by R. O. Kimmel (Appendix A) and used in Minnesota to allocate spring permits. Permits are allocated annually by TMU and season segment based on previous harvest, population trends, harvest goals, habitat quality, and hunter interference rates. The Minnesota system requires data on harvest, an independent index to population size, information on hunter effort and interference, and a subjective estimate of habitat quality.

The following procedures for regulating spring harvest where hunter numbers are controlled do not incorporate measures of hunter effort and habitat quality, but we indicate where those measures could be incorporated in the decision process.

1. Stratify the overall area into Turkey Management Units (TMUs).
Options include:
a. ecologically based units, e.g., physiographic regions.
b. political units, e.g., counties, townships.
c. combination of ecological and political units, e.g., aggregate counties to approximate physiographic units.

2. Establish hunting season segments.
Options include:
a. one season.
b. divide season into 2 or more segments, e.g., New Jersey has 5 sequential segments, each of which includes at least 1 Saturday.

3. Establish an annual harvest goal by TMU.
Options include:
a. minimal harvest density. This is the same approach taken where hunter numbers are unregulated. If harvest falls below the goal, permit numbers are reduced the following year in a predetermined way.
b. proportion of population. For example, Minnesota has established maximum harvest rate of 30% of the gobbler population. Population estimates are based on the previous spring kill. Permit quotas are established

for each TMU by considering trends in population, hunter success rates, habitat quality, and hunter interference rates (Appendix A). Note that this system also establishes a hunter density goal for each TMU.

4. Establish hunter density goals.
Options include:
a. no restrictions; all hunters are assigned the TMU they request.
b. maximum densities are established based on quality of hunt and safety considerations, e.g., 2 hunters/mile^2 of habitat; the number of permits for the TMU is equal to the area of habitat divided by the desired maximum number of hunters per mile^2.
c. hunter density based on harvest goals, see 3.b. above.

5. Measure harvest annually by TMU.
Options include one or more of the following:
a. mandatory check stations.
b. mandatory kill report card.
c. post-season surveys of hunters.

6. Monitor hunt quality as expressed by proportion of hunters experiencing interference by other hunters or numbers of hunters seen.
Options include:
a. post-season surveys.
b. mail back questionnaires with permit.

In the Minnesota system, hunter interference rates are used to create a weighting factor that can be used to increase or decrease the number of permits issued by TMU. These same surveys or questionnaires can be used to check kill reporting rates, estimates of hunter success derived from check stations or kill report cards, and hunter access problems on private land.

7. Obtain an annual index to population size that is independent of harvest.
Options include:
a. random surveys of hunters pursuing other species.
b. volunteer-cooperator reports.
c. staff/volunteer sighting records.

The Minnesota system (Appendix A) uses a population trend index based on the proportion of deer hunters observing wild turkeys in each of the last 3 years (Kimmel et al. 1996). Increasing trends yield a value >1 and decreasing trends yield a value <1. The trend index is used to adjust the harvest based population estimate for calculating permit allocations.

Additional Comments About Decision Variables

Harvest Rate
The model that we propose for regulating spring harvest assumes that harvest can be measured accurately, and that gobbler harvest is a valid index to population size. For the latter assumption to be true, hunters must remove a constant proportion of the population each spring (Steffen and Norman 1996). We recognize that variation in weather and other factors can cause variation in gobbler harvest rates that are independent from population size. Changes in hunter numbers or hunter effort are another important source of variation in harvest rate. A review of studies of spring gobbler harvest mortality (Vangilder 1992:156-157) confirms annual variation in gobbler harvest rate within sites and regional variation among sites. Testing the assumption that harvest rate is constant requires good estimates of population size. Recent, long-term studies conducted in Mississippi confirm that both gobbler harvest and harvest/unit of hunter effort provide reliable indices of population size and population trends (Lint et al. 1995). Gobbler harvest was the least expensive index to obtain.

To guard against uncontrolled sources of variation in gobbler harvest, we recommend collecting data on hunter effort and, if resources permit, obtaining an independent index of turkey abundance. Data on hunter numbers and effort can be used by management agencies for general planning purposes in addition to turkey harvest management. An independent index of population size adds validity to the management program regardless of the harvest strategy being used. Where hunter numbers are regulated, the population index can be used directly in the permit allocation process.

Juvenile: Adult Gobbler Age Ratios
We do not recommend using the ratio of juvenile to adult gobblers in the spring harvest as a basis for regulating harvest because much of the variation in this ratio seems unrelated to harvest rate. We do recommend, however, that agencies that collect age and weight data while recording harvest continue to do so. Hunters are especially interested in this type of descriptive data, and details about the harvest are useful when agencies communicate with hunters about turkey hunting and management programs.

Population modeling suggests that the percentage of adult males in the population will decrease as the overall harvest rate increases (Vangilder 1992:162). Thus, the ratio of adults to juveniles in the harvest should contain information about harvest rate. Some evidence suggests that when the proportion of adults in the spring harvest drops below 70%, the rate of harvest may be excessive (Paisley et al. 1996:42). Reported age ratios in the spring harvest, however, vary substantially among states (Kurzejeski and Vangilder 1992:188, Table 2), and show no clear relationship with season length or hunter effort.

Reported age ratios are affected by errors in data collection, annual population fluctuations, and hunter preferences for adult gobblers. Although juvenile and adult gobblers are readily distinguished, there seems to be considerable misclassification in data collected at cooperator run check stations or reported by hunters. Annual population fluctuations also influence spring harvest age ratios because the proportions of juveniles and adults in the population depend on the previous summer's reproduction. There is a higher proportion of juveniles in the spring population following years of good reproduction than following years of poor reproduction. Hunting traditions also seem to play a role because hunters from states such as Mississippi with long, liberal spring seasons harvest few juvenile gobblers (Miller 1997). In summary, age ratios of harvested birds are useful for describing the harvest, but much less useful than total harvest or harvest/hunter effort for regulating harvest.

Chapter 5. Spring Gobbler Harvest With Limited Either-Sex Fall Harvest

The general goals of this harvest strategy are to allow continued population growth, to protect and enhance spring gobbler hunting opportunities, and to provide additional recreation by allowing limited fall hunting. The emphasis is on spring gobbler hunting. Fall hunting is of secondary importance and fall hunting opportunities may be curtailed if the spring gobbler harvest declines. This limited fall harvest strategy is the model used by most northeastern states that have both spring and fall hunting seasons. The interest in and demand for fall hunting varies across the Northeast. Fall hunting traditions are well developed in New York, Pennsylvania, Virginia, and West Virginia; fall hunting pressure remains light in Connecticut and Massachusetts.

The conservative limited fall harvest strategy was designed in response to population sensitivity to either-sex harvest, annual fluctuations in fall population size that can exceed 50% of the long-term mean, and the increased risk of overharvest associated with poor mast crops and low poult production. Management experience and extensive research have demonstrated the sensitivity of turkey populations to fall either-sex harvest. Simulation modeling shows that fall harvests that remove less than 10% of the total population generally allow long-term population growth. Removals of more than 10% of the fall population invariably led to decreases in population size. Populations were sensitive to changes in adult hen mortality rates. When illegal loss of hens during the spring season was incorporated into these simulations, the "safe" fall harvest was between 5% and 10% of the total population. These simulations were based on extensive data from turkey populations in northern Missouri where over 7 spring seasons at least 5.2% of the radio-marked hens were shot illegally (Vangilder and Kurzejesky 1995). Rates of illegal hen loss were similar in Virginia and West Virginia (G. Norman and J. C. Pack, pers. commun.). In New York, the crude annual mortality rate attributed to human activity averaged 11.7% and ranged from 5.0% to 7.1% for radio-marked hens over 4 years (Roberts et al. 1995). These estimates include legal harvest and wounding, but poaching was the primary source of human induced mortality. Data are lacking for other northeastern states.

The limited fall-harvest strategy minimizes the risk of overharvest to an annually fluctuating population. The goal is to sustain a relatively constant fall harvest that is small enough to protect the population under worst-case conditions characterized by low reproduction and poor mast crops. No effort is made to exploit the larger fall populations that occur in years of better-than-average reproduction by liberalizing fall seasons. The limited fall harvest strategy has been successful in the Northeast.

Basic Assumptions

In contrast with spring gobbler hunting, biologists recognize that excessive either-sex harvests in the fall can slow population growth and cause populations to decline (Bailey and Rinell 1968). The decline of turkey populations during the eighteenth and nineteenth centuries has been attributed to a combination of habitat destruction and excessive harvest. The limited fall harvest strategy incorporates several new assumptions associated with 2 discrete harvest seasons and the removal of all age and sex classes. Here we review the new assumptions associated with limited fall harvest and discuss their relationship to the 4 assumptions underpinning spring gobbler harvest.

Assumption 1: Fall either-sex harvest affects population growth.

Simulation modeling suggests that harvesting 5-10% of the fall population will allow for continued population growth, but harvests exceeding 10% will usually lead to population decline. Spring and fall harvests are believed to be additive; illegal taking of hens during the spring season will reduce the allowable fall take (Vangilder and Kurzejeski 1995). The demographic factors that have the greatest effect on long-term population growth are nest success, hen survival, and poult survival (Vangilder and Kurzejeski 1995, Roberts and Porter 1996). Fall harvest strategies have a direct effect on hen survival; nest success and poult survival are not under the direct control of managers.

Regulations that control harvest rates and affect hen survival include limiting hunter numbers, season length, season timing in relation to seasons for other game species, and restrictions on hunting implement. Regulating hunter numbers with a permit system provides the greatest control over harvest. Where hunter numbers are not limited, shortening fall seasons has effectively reduced harvest rates. Experience with 11- to 12-week fall seasons in West Virginia has shown that harvest rates are greatest during the first week, decline steeply during the second week, and thereafter decline slowly. Thus, extended seasons add substantially to the total harvest. Shortening the West Virginia fall season to

5-6 weeks resulted in a rapid increase in turkey populations and fall harvest (Pack 1986).

Scheduling the opening of fall turkey season so it does not coincide with the opening date of other game seasons has also been effective at reducing harvest rates (Pack 1986). During concurrent seasons, and especially on opening days, much of the turkey harvest was associated with opportunistic taking by hunters pursuing other species. New Hampshire restricts fall turkey hunters to the use of archery equipment to minimize harvest while providing substantial recreational opportunity.

Assumption 2: Hunting mortality is additive to natural mortality.

This assumption was discussed under spring gobbler hunting (Chapter 4, Assumption 2). Here, we consider the additive interaction between fall and spring harvest. Gobblers removed during the fall season are unavailable for harvest the next spring. The direct effect of removing gobblers is less important than the effect that removing adult hens has on long-term population growth. In Virginia, there was no relationship between the annual fall harvest totals and the subsequent spring gobbler harvest over 10 consecutive years. There was a significant inverse relationship between the number of birds harvested/km^2 of forest in the fall and the growth rate of spring gobbler harvest over the same period. Spring gobbler harvest increased most rapidly (10.4% annually) where fall harvest was <0.1 bird/km^2 of forested habitat. At higher levels of fall harvest the annual growth rate in spring gobbler harvest was about 6%. An identical relationship was observed in an analysis of fall and spring harvest data from West Virginia (Steffen and Norman 1996). These results are consistent with population modeling predictions and confirm the need for conservative fall harvests where the program emphasis is on spring gobbler hunting.

Assumption 3: Turkey populations fluctuate annually.

The magnitude of annual fluctuations among northeastern turkey populations is illustrated in Figure 5.1 by a 10-year series of summer turkey sightings collected by conservation officers in Pennsylvania (W.E. Drake, unpubl. data). The total number of hens and poults observed in these state-wide surveys is significantly correlated with the subsequent fall harvest, and the counts provide a reliable index to fall population size (Wunz and Shope 1980, Wunz and Ross 1990). In this example, 4 years were "average" or within 5% of the 10-year mean. Two years (1984, 1989) were >25% below the 10-year mean, and 2 years (1987, 1990) were >25% above the 10-year mean. The largest count (1987) exceeded the 10-year mean by 40%, and the smallest count (1984) was 33% below the mean.

This strategy is designed to minimize the risk of overharvest in years when populations are well below average. In general, juvenile turkeys are more vulnerable to harvest than are adults. When reproductive success is high juveniles form the bulk

of the fall harvest (Steffen and Norman 1996). Conversely, when reproduction is poor, relatively fewer juveniles are harvested, thus the harvest must come largely from the adult component. The risk of overharvesting the adult hen population is usually greatest when fall populations are lowest.

Assumption 4: Vulnerability to harvest increases in years of poor mast production.

Although this assumption is commonly held by biologists, the evidence supporting it is mostly observational and correlational. The evidence that fall turkey harvests tend to increase in years of poor mast production and decrease when mast is abundant comes primarily from Pennsylvania and West Virginia where forests are extensive and fall hunting is a strong tradition (Wunz 1986, Pack 1994). For example, mast conditions were poor statewide in West Virginia in 1982 and the fall kill was among the highest on record. Gobbler harvests declined by 19% the following spring in counties open to fall hunting, but gobbler harvest increased by 52% in counties closed to fall hunting (Pack 1994).

The true relationship between harvest rate and mast abundance is unknown because turkey populations and mast crops are difficult to measure. In the Northeast, only Virginia, West Virginia, and Maryland conduct statewide mast surveys. The assumption that mast affects harvest is incorporated in the West Virginia fall harvest management model (Pack et al. 1995, Appendix B). At present, mast crops cannot be predicted until August or September and our basic understanding of the patterns of mast production among species and over time remains limited (Koenig et al. 1994, Healy 1997, Healy et al. 1999). Relationships among mast production and turkey populations merit further study because food resources affect seasonal movements and habitat use (Kurzejeski and Lewis 1990) and under some conditions, fall harvest (Menzel 1975, Wunz 1986, Pack 1994).

Fall Hunting Regulations

Season Dates and Season Length

In contrast to the biological basis for spring hunting seasons, fall seasons are determined largely by tradition. "Harvest of turkeys usually begins in October or November in the northern parts of the range, later in the southern portions. November was seemingly designed especially for turkey hunting" (Bailey and Rinell 1967:90). The regulations affecting fall turkey seasons in the Northeast are summarized in Table 5.1.

Season length has a significant effect on harvest. Most of the turkeys killed are taken on opening day, and daily kill diminishes rapidly through the second and third weeks. The daily kill then remains relatively constant for as long as the season continues (Bailey and Rinell 1968:35). Shortening fall hunting season has been effective at reducing harvest and permitting continued population growth (Pack 1986). Because most of the kill occurs early in the season a substantial

Figure 5.1. Variations in total number of wild turkey hens and poults observed by conservation officers in Pennsylvania during June, July, and August over a 10-year period, 1981-1990.

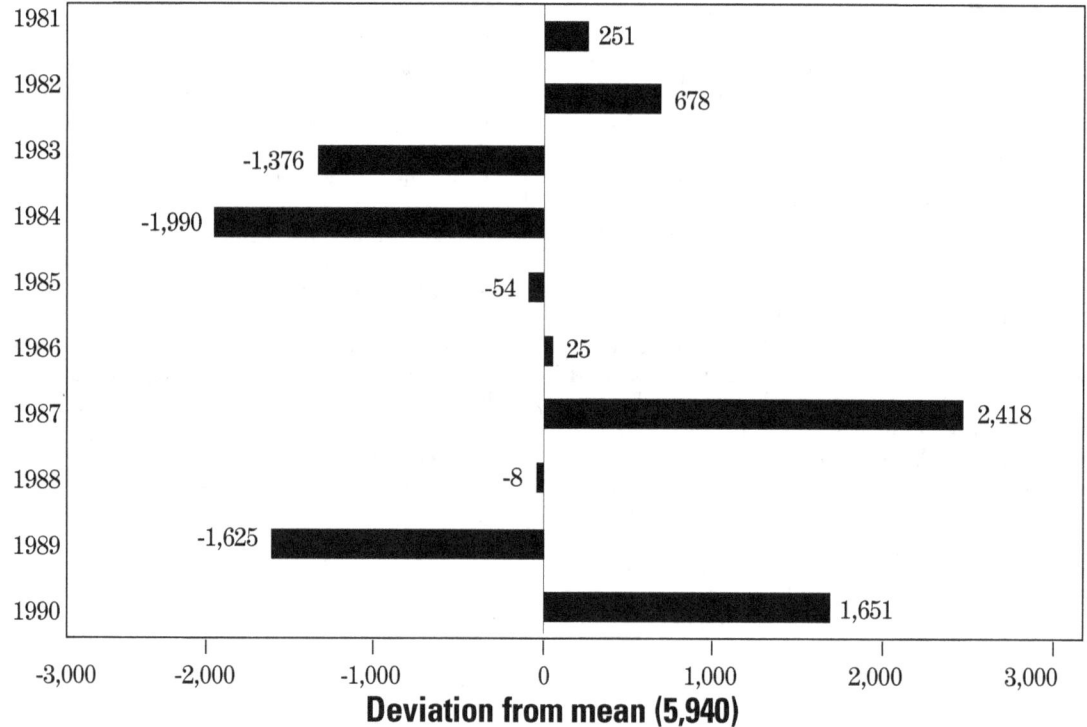

reduction in season length may be required to achieve a significant reduction in harvest. For example, in West Virginia, about half of the harvest occurred in the first week of an 11-week fall season. Reducing this season by 5 weeks would have reduced the kill by 20%, and shortening it 10 weeks would have reduced kill by 50% (Bailey and Rinell 1968:53). Fall firearms seasons for wild turkeys are either 1 or 2 weeks long in 8 northeastern states (Table 5.1). Thus ample opportunity exists to increase fall hunting opportunity, but the potential to reduce harvest by shortening the season is limited.

Timing of the season also affects harvest. When hunting seasons for turkey and other game species start at the same time, harvest is substantially increased because of increased hunter effort and opportunistic harvest of turkeys. Separating the start of turkey season from other hunting seasons has been effective at reducing harvest (Pack 1986). Snow fall during the late November seasons usually leads to increased harvest by enhancing the ability of hunters to locate flocks.

In the Northeast, fall seasons have generally been scheduled as late as possible to take advantage of the rapid growth of juvenile turkeys during autumn. A juvenile turkey harvested in mid-November will weigh about a pound more than one taken in mid-October. Season dates and length are pertinent to all 4 assumptions about fall harvest. Although adjusting season dates and length has been effective at providing a sustained fall harvest, these measures provide only weak control over harvest.

Bag Limits
Bag limits are pertinent to all 4 assumptions about fall either-sex harvest. In the Northeast, bag limits are generally 1 bird, but fall hunters may take 2 birds in parts of New York and Virginia. States with spring and fall hunts generally have an annual limit of 2 birds, only one of which can be taken in the fall. This regulation is believed to encourage spring hunting. In most states, little room exists to control fall harvest by manipulating bag limit.

Table 5.1 Regulations used for fall either-sex turkey seasons in the Northeast. Delaware, Maine, Ontario, and Rhode Island do not have fall seasons.

Regulation	CT	MD	MA	NH	NJ	NY	PA	VT	VA	WV
Season length, weeks										
Firearm or combination	2	1	1		<1[a]	2-7	1-2	2	2-8	2-4
Archery only	10			14				3	7	
Bag limit										
Firearms or combination	1	1[b]	1[b]		1	1-2	1	1[c]	2[d]	1[b]
Archery only	1			1				1[c]	2[d]	
Regulate hunter numbers										
None	x[e]	x	x[e]	x[e]		x[e]	x	x[e]		
Number					x					x[f]
Area				x[g]	x			x[g]		
Time										
Time and area										
Hunting implement										
Shotgun and shot size	x		x		x	x		x		
Archery gear	x		x	x	x	x		x		
Muzzle-loading shotgun		x				x				
Rifle, shotgun, bow		x						x	x	x
Harvest reporting										
Check station	x[h]	x	x	x	x			x	x	x
Report card	x[h]					x	x			

[a] Three-day fall turkey season in 1999.
[b] Bag limit: 2 bearded birds in spring season with no fall bird, or 1 bearded bird in spring and 1 bird of either sex in fall season.
[c] Combined fall bag limit of 1 for both the firearms and archery seasons.
[d] Bag limit: 1 per day, 3 per license year, no more than 2 of which may be taken in the fall or spring.
[e] Permit or license required, but numbers not restricted.
[f] Hunter numbers are regulated by permit in selected counties.
[g] Some management units are closed to turkey hunting.
[h] Successful fall firearms hunters must bring the bird to a check station; successful archery hunters must mail a report card within 24 hours of the kill.

Control of Hunter Numbers

Only 2 northeastern states, New Jersey and West Virginia, regulate hunter numbers with a permit system. West Virginia regulates fall turkey hunter numbers in management units that have recently been opened to hunting. Hunters in Connecticut are required to obtain written permission to hunt on private land, a practice that probably limits hunter numbers. Regulation of hunter numbers is pertinent to all assumptions about fall harvest.

Hunting Implement

Of the northeastern states, only New Hampshire uses restrictions on hunting gear as the method for limiting fall harvest. New Hampshire has a 14-week fall archery season and no fall firearms season; during 1994 bow hunters took 43 turkeys. Restrictions on hunting implement in other states are intended to promote safety. Five states (Conn., Mass., N.J., N.Y., Vt.) restrict hunters to shotguns and specific shot sizes. Connecticut and Vermont have separate fall firearms and archery seasons; Massachusetts, New Jersey, and New York permit shotguns and archery gear in fall seasons. Four states (Md., Pa., Va., W.Va.) allow the use of rifles in addition to shotguns and archery equipment.

Harvest Reporting

Biologists consider an accurate measure of harvest critical for management programs. Of the 10 states with fall seasons, 8 require successful hunters to bring birds to check stations. New York and Pennsylvania provide license holders with report forms to be returned by successful hunters. Reporting is mandatory in Pennsylvania and voluntary in New York. Compliance with reporting requirements varies geographically and temporally. All states consider non-reporting a serious source of error in harvest estimates and use either post-season mail or phone surveys to improve harvest estimates.

Decision Variables and Regulatory Procedures

Limited Fall Harvest, Hunter Numbers Regulated

This strategy requires regulating fall harvest in conjunction with spring harvest. Procedures for regulating spring gobbler harvest have been discussed, therefore we examine options for regulating fall, either-sex harvests in this section.

We recommend the strategy developed by the West Virginia Division of Natural Resources, Wildlife Resources Section to implement fall hunting in counties that had traditionally been hunted only in spring (Pack et al. 1995, Appendix B). This regulatory approach explicitly links fall harvest with spring harvest, controls harvest at the TMU level, and provides strong protection against overharvest.

The decision and regulatory process for a limited fall harvest is similar to that recommended for spring gobbler harvest where hunter numbers are controlled

(see Chapter 4). Spring gobbler harvest goals drive the decision process. Counties must meet a pre-established spring gobbler harvest-goal for 2 consecutive years to be opened to fall hunting, and counties are closed to fall hunting if the spring harvest goal is not met. The actual spring gobbler harvest is used to estimate population size. Hunter density is controlled with a permit system. Initial permit allocations are based on the population estimate, but permits are not issued until 1 October. Consequently, the final allocation can be adjusted in response to data from brood and mast surveys, which become available in September. The process depends on accurate measurement of the spring and fall harvest by TMU. Spring harvest must be tabulated promptly because it is used to estimate population size and the number of fall harvest permits to be issued.

The process used to regulate fall harvest is outlined below. We have generalized the process developed for West Virginia (Pack et al. 1995, Appendix B). Steps 1 and 2 are completed when the season is established, although TMU boundaries and harvest goals may be revised as the need arises. Steps 3 through 5 form an annual cycle of decision making and permit allocation.

Recommended Procedures

1. Stratify the overall area into Turkey Management Units (TMUs).
Options include:
a. ecologically based units, e.g., physiographic regions.
b. political units, e.g., counties, townships.
c. combination of ecological and political units, e.g., aggregate to approximate physiographic units.

The West Virginia model we are following uses counties as TMUs.

2. Establish spring harvest goals.
The spring harvest goal is the critical decision variable in this strategy and the factor that links fall with spring harvest. Minimum desirable spring harvest goals are established by TMU. Goals are based on long-term spring harvest records and goals are usually expressed as gobbler kill per unit area of wild turkey range. Fall hunts are permitted as long as the spring harvest equals or exceeds the established goal; fall hunting is curtailed if the spring harvest falls below the goal.

In West Virginia, the minimum spring gobbler harvest goal is 1 bird/mile^2 (0.4/km^2) of wild turkey range. Counties can be opened to fall either-sex hunting only when the spring gobbler harvest goal has been exceeded for 2 consecutive years. Counties are closed to fall hunting if the spring harvest goal is not met.

3. Establish fall harvest goals and permit allocations for each TMU.
Population size is estimated by assuming spring gobbler harvest is equal to 10% of the total population. Multiplying the population estimate by a desired harvest rate, usually 5-10%, produces the

target harvest. The number of permits required is estimated by dividing the target harvest by the estimated hunter success rate.

West Virginia uses a conservative harvest rate of 5% because illegal taking of hens is known to be a problem. Hunter success rates are estimated from harvest report data, and West Virginia currently uses a fall hunter success rate of 0.27.

The timing of the permit allocation process is important. In West Virginia, spring gobbler harvest data are compiled by June and counties that will be open to fall hunting are identified. Harvest goals and permit allocations are then established and fall permit applications are available by 1 July. Fall harvest permits are mailed no later than 1 October for a late October hunting season. Permit allocations seldom change after 1 July, but the late mailing date allows biologists the option of changing allocations after reviewing summer brood reports and mast condition information that becomes available in September.

4. Measure harvest annually by TMU.
Options include one or more of the following:
a. mandatory check stations. This is the option used in West Virginia.
b. mandatory kill report card.
c. post-season surveys of hunters.

5. Obtain an annual index to population size that is independent of harvest.
Options include:
a. random surveys of hunters pursuing other species.
b. volunteer-cooperator reports.
c. staff-volunteer sightings records.

There are 2 ways that independent indices to population size can be used to strengthen the manager's hand in regulating limited fall harvests. The first is to provide a check on spring harvest data, which are used as the decision variable on whether to hunt in the fall and also serve as the basis for the population estimate. This is the approach we recommended under "Spring gobbler harvest, hunter numbers regulated," where we described the process used in Minnesota (Appendix A). In the Minnesota model, spring gobbler harvest is assumed to equal 10% of the total population. The population estimate is then multiplied by a trend index derived from a random sample of antlerless deer permit holders. The trend is defined by changes in the proportion of deer permit holders observing turkeys over the past 3 years.

The second way an independent index can be used is to adjust the fall permit quota. In this case, data from summer brood counts are used to index fall population size. This approach has been selected in West Virginia where managers have the option of changing fall permit quotas in response to summer brood sighting data. The West Virginia system is new and formal decision rules have not been developed. With experience, formal rules can be developed. For example, permit quotas could be increased when

brood counts were >25% above the long-term mean. Alternatively, permit quotas could be decreased in proportion to the decline in brood counts when brood counts were >25% below the long-term mean.

Limited Fall Harvest, No Control on Hunter Numbers

The strategy of limited fall harvest has also been successfully implemented without any control over hunter numbers. Where hunter numbers are unregulated, fall harvests have been limited to a level that allows continued population growth by regulating season length, season timing, and bag limit. Of these 3 regulations, season length has the greatest effect on total harvest. In general, states that traditionally had extended fall seasons were able to increase rates of population growth, as indexed by spring gobbler kill, by shortening fall seasons (Pack 1986). The length of fall firearms seasons in states without control over hunter numbers currently ranges from 1 to 9 weeks. Shorter seasons are the rule where hunting pressure is greatest.

The scheduling of fall turkey season relative to seasons for other game species also has a significant effect on harvest rate. In West Virginia, band recovery rates for wild turkeys in the fall season ranged from 15% to 23% during a 10-year period when turkey and squirrel seasons opened concurrently. During the decade after fall turkey season started 2 weeks later than squirrel season, the band recovery rates of marked birds varied from 1.6% to 6.2% (Pack 1994).

Bag limits for fall seasons are usually 1 bird/hunter. The general practice is to have an annual limit of 2 turkeys, only one of which can be taken in the fall. The option of allowing hunters to take both birds in the spring is intended to encourage spring harvest. Another effective approach to providing fall hunting recreation while limiting harvest has been to restrict hunters to the use of archery gear.

Procedures for Regulating Limited Fall Harvest Without Controlling Hunter Numbers

Except for establishing fall harvest and permit goals, we recommend the same procedures used when hunter numbers are regulated. Again, spring harvest goals and an accurate measurement of spring and fall harvests are critical features of the system. Specifying remedial actions to be taken when spring harvest goals are not met is more difficult when hunter numbers are unregulated. The procedure is outlined below, but we will elaborate only where the process differs from the previous one.

1. Establish Turkey Management Units (TMUs).

2. Establish long-term spring harvest goals for each TMU, and specify remedial actions to be taken if harvest falls below the goal.

We recommend expressing spring harvest goals as kill/unit of habitat, and basing them on program goals and past harvest records. Where hunter numbers are uncontrolled, the options for restricting fall harvest include adjusting season length, season timing, bag limits, and hunting implement. Season length and season timing have proven effective on the long-term maintenance of fall harvest objectives. Adjusting season length may be the only practical option for a

short-term response to declining spring harvest. For example, fall seasons would remain unchanged as long as spring harvest goals were met. If the spring harvest goal was not met, the following fall season would be shortened, or stopped altogether, until the spring harvest goal was again achieved. Clearly, the option of regulating fall hunter density should be considered as a response to declining spring harvests.

3. Measure harvest annually by TMU.

4. Obtain an annual index to population size that is independent of harvest.

Combining Regulatory Procedures for the Spring-Plus-Limited-Fall-Harvest Strategy

The regulatory procedures outlined so far can be combined in 4 ways to implement the spring-plus-limited-fall-harvest strategy. Each combination of procedures provides a different degree of control over harvest. The greatest control over harvest and protection against excessive harvest is obtained by regulating hunter numbers in both spring and fall seasons. The least control over harvest occurs when hunter numbers are unregulated in both seasons. The general relationships between regulation of hunter numbers and control over harvest are shown in Table 5.2.

The choice of regulatory procedures depends on the perceived risk of overharvest and the degree of

emphasis placed on spring versus fall hunting by the management agency. Different combinations of regulatory procedures can be used within a state. For example, West Virginia uses 2 distinct regulatory approaches to implement the same harvest strategy. In the region of West Virginia where turkeys were never extirpated and fall hunting has a long tradition, biologists chose not to restrict hunter numbers in either spring or fall seasons. Where turkey populations have recently been restored, biologists have chosen a more conservative approach and regulate hunter numbers in the fall seasons but not in the spring.

In addition to allowing greater control over harvest, procedures that regulate hunter numbers also allow prompt management response to changes in harvest and population status. This is an important distinction between regulatory procedures that affect hunter numbers and those that do not. Regulating hunter numbers allows managers to make immediate, incremental changes in response to harvest and population data. Where hunter numbers are uncontrolled, managers are limited to making structural changes in seasons, such as shortening seasons or changing opening dates and bag limits. Populations respond slowly to these kinds of regulatory changes and at least 5 years is required to assess their effect on populations (Weaver and Mosby 1979). Making structural changes in hunting seasons is often difficult because hunters tend to resist changes (Wunz 1986). Once a permitting system has been established, adjusting permit quotas becomes a routine administrative procedure. Regulating hunter numbers allows a constant season structure while controlling hunter effort.

Table 5.2. General relationships among procedures that regulate hunter numbers, degree of control over harvest, and risk of overharvest.

Control of harvest	Risk of overharvest	Hunter numbers regulated		Example
		Spring hunt	Fall hunt	
Greatest	Least	Yes	Yes	New Jersey
		No	Yes	W.Va., newly occupied range
		Yes	No	
Least	Greatest	No	No	Va. and W.Va., historic range

Chapter 6. Maximize Combined Spring and Fall Harvests

This strategy represents an effort to derive the maximum harvest from a fluctuating population without diminishing population growth rate. This strategy is based on the same assumptions and uses the same hunting regulations as the previously described spring and fall harvest strategies. Material on assumptions and hunting regulations will not be repeated.

Maximizing the total spring and fall turkey harvest is similar to maximum sustained-yield approaches used for other species, but the turkey model differs in important ways. Most maximum sustained-yield models assume a constant carrying capacity and density-dependent population responses that cause the population to grow toward carrying capacity whenever it has been displaced. The models envision a relatively stable system, with self-regulating mechanisms that cause the population to oscillate around a mean value. In contrast, we assume that turkey populations are volatile, routinely fluctuating by 50% or more around long-term mean levels. Density-dependent population responses have not been identified for turkeys, and the available population models do not assume density-dependent population growth (Chapter 3). No explicit assumptions have been made about carrying capacity, but we recognize that variations in weather and mast production affect turkey populations in ways that are independent of population density.

For wild turkeys, a fixed harvest rate will result in annually fluctuating harvests. A fixed harvest quota based on mean fall population size would result in under- or overharvest about as often as it would produce a desired harvest (Fig. 5.1). Optimizing total harvest requires an estimate or index of population size just prior to harvest and a means for regulating hunter numbers after the population estimate is available. Obtaining reliable indices of population size and regulating hunter numbers just prior to hunting is often administratively impractical.

Two potential models for optimizing fall harvest are available from the Northeast. In Pennsylvania, biologists capitalized on years of good reproduction by extending fall seasons when summer brood counts were >25% above the 10-year mean for the management unit. Seasons were initially set at 1 or 2 weeks with the option of extending them depending on the results of summer brood counts. Season extensions were announced in September. This system was used because hunter numbers were uncontrolled.

It did provide additional recreation and harvest in years when turkeys were abundant.

The current system used in West Virginia to limit fall harvest could also be used to optimize fall harvest. Hunter numbers are regulated. Populations are estimated from spring gobbler harvest; permit allocations are based on a 5% maximum harvest and 27% success rate. Biologists can review brood and mast survey data before making the final allocation of permits on 1 October. This system contains all the elements needed to obtain a fixed fall harvest rate.

Maximizing the combined annual spring and fall harvest would involve combining the regulatory procedures we have outlined for spring and fall harvests where hunter numbers are regulated. Hunter numbers would be regulated in both spring and fall and permit allocations would be based on population estimates. The permit allocation process would follow the guidelines developed in Minnesota (Appendix A) and West Virginia (Appendix B).

Those procedures have already been described in detail, so we will only outline the annual decision process.

1. Establish spring harvest goals.
Population estimate is based on previous spring harvest adjusted by an independent population trend index.

2. Establish hunter density goals.
This step is used to provide as much hunting opportunity as possible when the demand for permits exceeds the supply. The season is divided into segments and a maximum hunter density goal is used to partition the permit quota among hunting season segments.

3. Measure spring harvest.
Includes estimating hunter interference rates.

4. Establish fall harvest goals and permit allocations.
Based on spring harvest, desired harvest rate, and estimated hunter success rate.

5. Obtain index to late summer population size.
Based on summer brood counts.

6. Adjust fall permit allocation in response to brood surveys.

7. Measure fall harvest.

8. Obtain index of fall population size. Random surveys of deer hunters or volunteer/cooperator surveys such as the West Virginia Bow Hunter Survey. This index is used to adjust the spring population estimate.

Maximizing the total harvest has some stringent requirements for data and regulations. There must be an estimate of population size in late summer and a means of regulating season structure or hunter numbers in September before the hunt. The West Virginia model shows how those tasks can be accomplished. We also believe that maximizing the total harvest would require regulating hunter numbers in spring and obtaining a second index to population size in late fall. It is not clear to us that there is enough demand to implement the maximum harvest strategy even in the states of Virginia, West Virginia, and New York where fall hunting is popular.

Section IV. Techniques

Chapter 7. Introduction to Population Estimation

Why Measure Abundance?

Three types of information are needed to manage wildlife populations: (a) total numbers, (b) population dynamics, and (c) distributions and movements (Norton-Griffiths 1978). In this chapter we focus on estimating population size. "The future ability of researchers and managers to provide for more detailed evaluations of the impacts of both habitat management practices and harvest regulations on turkey populations requires the means to detect changes in population size" (Kurzejeski and Vangilder 1992). Understanding population dynamics requires knowledge of the population size (Verner 1985), thus population dynamics and abundance estimation are linked. Population models that project changes in numbers over time require an initial estimate of population size (see Fig. 3.1). Many management programs for wild turkeys include provisions for removing a fixed percentage of the population each hunting season (Mosby 1967, Hayden and Wunz 1975), thus requiring estimation of the pre-hunting population size. However, estimating animal abundance presents many problems, especially for species like wild turkeys that are inconspicuous, mobile, and wide ranging (Bull 1981). It is difficult to know what proportion of the population is detectable and be sure that the same proportion of the population is detected each time the technique is used. Thus, counts need to be standardized to ensure comparable results (Davis and Winstead 1980:224).

Census, Estimate, and Index

The term *census* is often used to refer to any abundance estimation technique (e.g., Caughley and Sinclair 1994). It is strictly defined, however, as a complete count of all individuals in a given population, such as all the wild turkeys inhabiting a state, or all wild turkeys at a particular winter roosting site. In contrast, a *survey* samples some proportion of the individuals in a population. An *estimate* is derived from a sample of the overall population, which can be extrapolated to the overall population size or density by using various statistical or mathematical manipulations. An estimate is an approximation of the true population size and may be subject to varying degrees of bias. An *index* is any measurable factor presumed to be related to population size in some way. The index changes in a predictable manner with changes in population size, but does not estimate it directly. An index is used because this factor is easier to count than the animal itself. It may be possible to convert or "calibrate" the index to the true population size, if a suitable proportionality constant or correction factor can be determined (McClure 1939; Overton and Davis 1969:415; Eberhardt 1978a:213; Davis and Winstead 1980:231; Bull 1981; Seber 1982:54-55,451). The correction factor, however, is rarely known, or the proportionality may be variable. An index is a measure of *relative abundance* that is useful for comparing the relative size of a population among different areas, years, or seasons. A census or estimate, in contrast, is a measure of *absolute abundance.*

An index may be direct or indirect (Bull 1981). A *direct index* is obtained by using a sampling scheme to count the animals. Although animals are counted directly, a direct population estimate does not result. An example would be the numbers of turkeys seen per kilometer of road driven, or reports of numbers of turkeys seen by deer hunters. An *indirect index* involves factors associated with the presence of the animals, such as tracks or dens.

The main advantage of a census is that if the procedure is done accurately, it produces the actual population size, not an estimate subject to error. A census may be easier to explain and defend in court than a method that extrapolates abundance from a sample, or an index of relative abundance (Weinrich et al. 1985). A census makes the assumptions that (1) the entire area is searched, (2) all groups of animals are located, and (3) all groups are counted accurately (Norton-Griffiths 1978:5). These assumptions are difficult to meet under field conditions. All animals in the population are not equally visible (Eberhardt et al. 1979), and counting errors can be a significant source of bias. Animal behavior and movements may compound counting errors, and complete coverage is difficult for large areas (Caughley 1977a). As a result, most censuses are subject to some unknown degree of error. Furthermore, censuses can be prohibitively expensive, or technically impossible for large areas. Because wild turkeys are elusive and distributed among diverse cover types censusing the birds is generally impractical (Donohoe et al. 1983). Still, a census may be feasible for a small area, in a habitat where turkeys are easily seen.

The main advantage of estimates is that every individual need not be counted to obtain an estimate of abundance. Sampling procedures can be used to greatly reduce the effort, time, and cost of the project. Problems caused by duplicate counts or missed individuals may be greatly reduced compared with a census, and an estimate need not be completed in a short time (Caughley 1977a:25). Many sources of error in estimates must be accounted for or controlled, however, and obtaining reliable samples may be difficult. Because it is often difficult to reveal the magnitude or sources of these errors, the resulting population estimate may be inaccurate. Nevertheless, if a population size need only be known within a certain confidence level (e.g., ±10%), then a sample will usually suffice. The cost and manpower required for a complete census make estimates the only feasible alternative for determining the population size of most wildlife species.

Often, knowing the actual population size is unnecessary. In many management programs it is more important to know about trends among seasons or years, or whether one area has more or fewer individuals than another. In these situations, an index is appropriate. Caughley (1977a:14) advised that, "a problem defined in terms of absolute density can usually be redefined in such a way that estimates by relative density will provide a solution." Relative methods are adequate for many problems, and they should be used when adequate because they are much easier and less costly than absolute methods (Krebs 1989). Indices are frequently used to monitor state and regional population trends (Kurzejeski and Vangilder 1992:171), and they are generally adequate to manage wildlife populations (Caughley 1977a:14). An index may be considerably less expensive and labor-intensive than either an estimate or a census because indices can be obtained from observations by volunteers or cooperators (Welsh and Kimmel 1990, Applegate 1997). Furthermore, an index may have a smaller variance than the corresponding population estimate (Eberhardt and Simmons 1987). Indices have the additional advantage that they cause minimal disturbance to the animals. An index may be the only practical method in situations where obtaining accurate counts of animals is difficult. Indices may be sufficient, or even necessary, if the only goal is to determine the distribution of a species in an area or across a state (Hoffman 1962).

Indices, however, have several disadvantages. Indirect indices are not time-specific because animal sign may have been left over a long period. Because counts of sign index abundance over time rather that at a specific time, indirect indices may be less reliable than direct counts (Caughley 1977a). Indices cannot be used for management decisions that require absolute numbers. A serious problem can arise if the relationship between index and population size varies over time or with the size of the population (Eberhardt and Simmons 1987). Differences among observers can affect data and make it necessary to evaluate variation among participants in the survey (Davis and Winstead 1980:231). Typically, a sampling procedure needs to be developed to collect data because large areas cannot be searched entirely. It is just as important to consider sampling design for indices as for estimates, and replicate samples should be obtained to calculate sampling estimates of variances (Seber 1982:451, 564).

White et al. (1982:32) took an extreme view of indices, saying that "the use of indices in science is to be discouraged because indices lack the basic factors required for making inferences about parameters based on data. Indices are useful only when they have been calibrated with the parameter of interest by using, for example, the theory of double sampling...." Seber (1982:54) considered indices generally less reliable than direct methods of abundance estimation. Indices are based on the difficult-to-prove assumption that the ratio of the index to the true population size is the same among the different localities, years, or populations being compared (Davis and Winstead 1980). An index is useful only if it is relatively stable under varying environmental conditions, and should therefore be carefully studied to examine this stability (Seber 1986). According to Lancia et al. (1994), "use of indices is often restricted to comparisons between populations on the same area over time or between different areas at the same time, because the exact relationship between the index and the true population frequently is not known."

Table 7.1 lists the population abundance techniques that we evaluated and indicates which techniques are treated as censuses, estimates, or indices. The assignment of a technique into one of these 3 categories is not always clear-cut. A given technique may be used to census one subspecies or habitat type and to estimate or index abundance in other situations. For example, counting wild turkeys at roosts may be an accurate census for the Rio Grande subspecies in Texas, where the habitat is open and turkeys congregate in specific areas for roosting. In other regions, it may be possible to census accurately a given flock (a partial census) in winter, although there may be uncounted individuals or flocks in the area. Such counts could provide an index if the size of a flock or the combined count of all known flocks is related to the size of the overall population (Caughley and Sinclair 1994:191).

Aerial counts may also be classified in different ways. For some species, such as large mammals in an open habitat, a thorough search can locate all individuals present. In most cases, however, the cost of completely surveying a large area can be prohibitive. Furthermore, in some areas or for some species, an aerial count may fail to account for all animals present, due to hidden animals or observer errors. It is usually necessary to sample a portion of the available habitat and correct for the unobservable fraction of the population, in which case the aerial count is at best an estimate, or at worst an index. This point is illustrated by Krebs (1989:103), who states that "in some cases the biases may remain of unknown magnitude, and aerial counts should then *not* be used as absolute population estimates."

Scales of Abundance

Abundance can be measured at several scales (Verner 1985:248). Proper study design depends on selecting an appropriate scale. A nominal scale records presence or absence. This scale might be useful for distribution studies, or for frequency indices. An *ordinal scale* ranks populations in the correct order of abundance, and might be used for an index that ranks study areas, or years for the same study area, from most to least abundant. A *ratio scale* assumes that all groups are sampled equally (i.e., the same percentage of the animals present are detected), and therefore allows relative percentages to be calculated. For example, management area A has 25% more turkeys/km^2 than management area B has, or the turkey population is 25% higher than last year's. Because the ratio scale does not require actual population numbers, it is a measure of relative abundance, or an index. It is an appropriate scale for studying annual or seasonal population trends. Finally, an *absolute scale* assumes a total count, or at least accurate correction coefficients for adjusting a biased count to the actual numbers in the population. A census produces an absolute count directly, whereas an estimate approximates the absolute count by extrapolation of a sampled area to the overall population. At least a ratio scale of abundance is needed to address most study objectives (Verner 1985:251). An absolute scale is indicated if the objective is measuring population fluctuations, or for determining the actual size of the population of a given area.

Parameters, Techniques, and Tools

The terms *parameter* and *technique* have not been used consistently when applied to methods for wild turkey management. A *parameter* is defined as a fixed or true quantity (a constant) characterizing a given population, expressed as a number (White et al. 1982:7, Lancia et al. 1994:216), which may be entered into a population model. Examples of parameters include true population size, population density, age-specific survival rate, average clutch size, fecundity, sex ratio, or capture probability. Because the values of parameters are seldom known, we generally use an *estimator*, "a mathematical expression that indicates how to calculate an estimate of a parameter from the sample data" (White et al. 1982:16). A *technique* is a field or statistical method for measuring this parameter. We will also refer to a *tool* as some facilitator of the main techniques that does not estimate or index population abundance in itself, but assists with the implementation of the technique. A tool can either be a physical piece of equipment, such as a camera, a tape recorder, or a postcard questionnaire sent to hunters, or some specific modification of a technique, such as the use of mail carriers to facilitate roadside counts, which are normally done by agency personnel.

Population Index, Density Index, and Production Index

In publications discussing animal abundance, the terms "abundance index/estimate" and "density index/estimate" are often used as if they were equivalent concepts. This usage is understandable, because density is simply population size divided by area occupied. It would seem that as long as the area being sampled was known, then both abundance and density would be known. However, calculating density becomes complicated when the area sampled is not the same as the area from which the animals are drawn (White et al. 1982:120). For example, in the case of animals with well-defined home ranges, a line of traps may barely intersect an animal's home range that lies mostly outside the study plot. The area from which the animals were drawn therefore includes additional area outside the study plot encompassing every home range intersecting the study plot boundary. Furthermore, traps on the edge of the study plot tend to catch many immigrants. This "edge effect" may result in a severe overestimate of the actual population density (Dice 1938, Seber 1982:446). Thus, the calculated area of the study plot may need to be adjusted by adding a "boundary strip" to the perimeter (White et al. 1982:120). Furthermore, the area of the sample plot may include habitat unsuitable for the species being surveyed. For example, a study plot for a terrestrial species that includes a lake covering 30% of the plot would be only 70% occupiable habitat. This distinction is the difference between *absolute density*, or population size divided by the absolute size of the area sampled, and *ecological density*, or population size divided by the total area of *suitable* habitat within the area sampled (Brower 1990).

Density may be the most appropriate measure for many comparisons (Caughley 1977a:12, Eberhardt 1978a), but it is more difficult to estimate than population size (White et al. 1982:3). Population estimates from different-sized areas cannot be compared directly. Density estimates are more useful for making ecological comparisons between populations occupying different size ranges. If the objective is to compare a population in a *given* area among years or seasons, or to track population trends over time, a measure of abundance may work as well as, or better than a measure of density. Density is sampled "by dividing the area under survey into sampling units and counting animals on a pre-selected proportion of these. The mean density per unit sampled is taken as an estimate of the mean density on sampled and unsampled units combined" (Caughley 1977a:25). When boundary effects or ecological density are not at issue, average density, as estimated from the sample areas, can be multiplied by the total area occupied by the population to produce an estimate of the total population size (Seber 1982:20).

Sometimes the objective is to index population parameters such as reproduction, rather than population abundance or density. Reproduction (Fig. 3.1) is one of the main parameters related to population size, and studying reproduction may provide insight into population trends. A *production index* is used to index reproductive parameters. Production indices "are valuable in assessing population status and evaluating harvest strategies" (Kurzejeski and Vangilder 1992:173). Because some techniques used to index abundance also serve to index production, separating these 2 types of techniques into distinct groups is difficult. Some techniques simultaneously produce information on abundance and production. Roadside counts, for example, may record the total number of turkeys seen or heard, and numbers of poults, hens, and broods observed. The total number of turkeys or broods seen may provide an index of abundance, whereas average brood size, poult:hen ratios, or percent of hens without poults may be used for production indices (Mosby 1967:126, Beasom 1970). The total number of broods seen may produce *both* an index of abundance and a separate index of productivity.

Assumptions

Every abundance estimation method rests on a number of assumptions. Where mathematical or statistical models are employed, these assumption are explicitly stated. In other methods, these assumptions may not be clearly defined, but they are nonetheless important. For example, a winter flock count, as a census technique, does not require statistical models or mathematical calculations other than addition. It is assumed, however, that no animals are missed or counted twice. Assumptions in more rigorous models are important because they take the place of additional parameters that would otherwise need to be measured to make the technique valid. For example, the line transect technique incorporates the assumption that all animals present directly on the survey line are counted with probability 1.0. As long as there is no reason to doubt that this assumption is valid, there is no need to measure this probability before the technique can be used. The more assumptions a model makes, the fewer parameters need to be measured in the field.

Two basic assumptions from Davis and Winstead (1980:222) must be considered for any population estimation method. First, "mortality and recruitment during the period when data are collected are negligible, or if not, are corrected in the estimates." Second, "all members of the population have an equal, or known, probability of being counted." Because many population estimating techniques violate one or both of these assumptions to varying degrees, the choice of method should be carefully considered before collecting data to minimize potential violations of the assumptions. According to Seber (1982:561), "if there is likely to be any question about the validity of the underlying assumptions, the sample data should be collected in such a way that the empirical variance estimates are available for replicated samples. A comparison of the sampling variance with the estimated theoretical variance predicted by the model will often throw some light on the validity of the model."

As the number of assumptions increases, the more likely it is that at least one of them will be violated.

Some assumptions are more critical than others, and most estimation techniques are sensitive to the violation of certain assumptions (White et al. 1982). If a non-critical assumption is seriously violated, or if a critical assumption is violated in a minor way, the model may become invalid and produce unreliable abundance estimates, or alternatively, it may produce results similar to those that would have been produced if the assumptions were strictly followed. If a model can tolerate some deviations from the assumptions and produce reliable results, the model is considered *robust*. Robust models are preferable to non-robust models, but there may be little choice if the robust methods are prohibitively expensive or are inappropriate for a given species or habitat.

Bias, Accuracy, Precision, and Sample Size

Population abundance techniques vary in their accuracy and consistency. *Accuracy* refers to how close an estimate is to the true population size or density. Inaccurate estimates are *biased*, where bias is the difference between the true size of the population and the estimate when repeated many times. Bias is an error in a constant direction. It is one of two general types of error, the other being normal sampling variation (Norton-Griffiths 1978:37).

Precision refers to how repeatable an estimate is if it is measured several times independently. Precision can be optimized by careful experimental design (Seber 1982:454), but accuracy may be difficult to control if the magnitude and direction of bias is unknown. A population estimate can be accurate (and therefore unbiased) but imprecise if several estimates of the same population vary widely, even though the average of the estimates is close to the true population size. Conversely, a population estimate can be precise but inaccurate (therefore biased) if several estimates of the same population are close to each other, but on average are far from the true population size.

Another important consideration is the sample size needed to produce a reliable abundance estimate or detect changes of a certain magnitude—generally, the larger the sample size, the better the accuracy and precision of the estimate. When animals occur in a clumped distribution, more plots must usually be sampled to produce an accurate estimate of density (Caughley 1977a:26-27). If there is bias in the data that cannot be corrected, increasing sample size will have little effect on accuracy. For example, if males are consistently more difficult to observe than other subgroups, every estimate, no matter how many repetitions are done, will be an underestimate. Estimating sample size is complicated because the magnitude or direction of existing bias is rarely known (Bibby et al. 1992:34). Excessive sampling wastes resources, and a balance must be sought between quality of results and available resources (Cochran 1977:72). Robson and Regier (1964) suggested 3 standards for accuracy in determining population size, depending on management objectives: (1) for preliminary surveys, where only a rough idea of population size is needed, accuracy of ±50% is sufficient; (2) for management work, where a moderate level of accuracy is desired, ±25% is recommended; (3) for research where accurate data are needed, ±10% is recommended.

Most estimation techniques have such low precision that only large changes in the population can be detected (Davis and Winstead 1980). According to Caughley (1977b) "appropriate sampling techniques coupled with standardized methods of survey ensure that even if our estimates are inaccurate at least they are repeatable. At worst they will be usable as indices of density, if not measures of absolute density." Seber (1982:458) also recommended handling the inaccuracy of estimation methods by recognizing that the estimates are biased and treating them as relative rather than absolute measures of abundance. Bias can be held constant by rigorously standardizing the methods, and the indices obtained can be used for monitoring changes in the population size and distribution, and determining preferences for different habitats. Similarly, Krebs (1989:58-59) points out that "biased estimates may be better than no estimates, but you should be careful to use these estimates only as *indices* of population size. If the bias is such as to be consistent over time, your biased estimates may be reliable indicators of changes in a population."

Estimation methods with both high accuracy and high precision can be very expensive (Davis and Winstead 1980:222). It may be preferable to sacrifice either accuracy or precision to attain a study design that will produce acceptable results for the purpose in mind. Accuracy is more important for obtaining an abundance estimate if a population is to be reduced by culling, or if biomass estimates are of interest. In contrast, precision is more important when repeated abundance estimates will be used to monitor trends over time, although bias must also remain constant among censuses (Norton-Griffiths 1978:41-42, Rabinowitz 1993:120). However, both accuracy and precision should be considered even if one is more important than the other for a given management objective, or if it is only possible to maximize one of the two.

Sources of bias include (1) skill of observer, (2) conspicuousness of animal, (3) weather conditions, (4) species activity related to time of day or season, (5) duplicate counts of individuals driven ahead by flushing, (6) variation of the screening effect of habitat, and (7) distance from the observed animal (Brower 1990:120). Verner (1985:254-259) discusses these factors in detail, and adds various effects of study design as an additional source of bias.

Observability and Sampling

Observability and *sampling* must be considered in any abundance estimation project (Lancia et al. 1994:218). Most abundance estimating methods do not account for all animals present. It is necessary to

estimate the proportion of the animals observed to develop a proportionality constant for transforming the count into an estimate of abundance. Limitations of time and money usually prohibit a survey from being conducted over the entire study area (Lancia et al. 1994:218). Several decisions must be made to deal with the problems of observability and sampling. The first decision is whether the study area is large enough to require sampling instead of a complete census. Decisions must then be made about the size and number of plots, and a sampling scheme, such as stratified random sampling or simple random sampling, must be selected (Lancia et al. 1994:247).

Selection of an Abundance Estimation Method

A wide selection of census, estimate, and index techniques is available. Choosing the "best" method depends largely on the management or study objectives (Järvinen 1976, Eberhardt 1978a, Verner 1985:249), which should be clearly defined beforehand. Absolute estimates may be necessary if a population is managed for maximum sustained-yield harvesting or to limit abundance to a specific level (Bull 1981, Seber 1982:458, Eberhardt and Simmons 1987). Measures of relative density may be sufficient for studies of habitat use, rate of increase, dispersal, and responses of the population to manipulation (Bull 1981). Absolute estimates are also necessary for studies where population density is to be related to behavior, reproductive rate, survival, emigration, or immigration (Caughley 1977a). Complete counts will usually be unattainable, thus an estimate will have to be used. Choice of estimating technique will depend on available manpower and funding. Estimating techniques that provide the most accurate and consistent results may be prohibitively expensive, and the most expensive and labor-intensive techniques do not necessarily always produce the most reliable results. Each technique should be reviewed to determine (1) how critical the assumptions are and the consequences of a departure from these assumptions, and (2) whether the assumptions are valid for the subspecies and habitat type under consideration.

After selection of a potential technique, it may be desirable to conduct a pilot study to test for violations of the assumptions, and determine if the variance of the estimates is within acceptable limits for the expected sample size. The accuracy or precision needed will depend on management objectives. If trends, rather than actual numbers, are all that is desired, then an index may suffice. As with estimates, some indices are more reliable than others given the species or habitat under consideration, and some will not be feasible given the cost or manpower required. The selection of a method will also depend on habitat and landscape characteristics (Stauffer 1993), the size of the area, and how the species is distributed throughout the habitat (Seber 1982:560). Finally, the selection of a method should depend on the techniques' advantages and disadvantages, and how they relate to wild turkey ecology and behavior. Krebs

(1989:12) presents a flowchart for selecting an appropriate method based on the factors discussed above. Caughley and Sinclair (1994:190) and Bibby et al. (1992:22-23) also provide lists of questions to be considered before selecting a suitable method. After considering all these factors, one might construct a list of several potentially suitable methods. It would be preferable, resources permitting, to use more than one estimating method simultaneously and then compare the results (Rusch and Keith 1971).

There is no general agreement as to which abundance estimation technique is best for wild turkeys (Welsh and Kimmel 1990). There is probably no completely reliable technique for estimating turkey abundance over extensive areas of eastern forest habitat (Mosby 1967, Wise 1973). Existing methods for inventorying wild turkey populations need further evaluation and development (Wunz and Ross 1990). In attempting to determine which of the many available techniques is "best," we suggest following Pollock and Kendall's (1987:509) thinking: "the question here should not be which of the techniques . . . is the best, but which one is the best to be used, given the population, the species, the habitat, the budget, and the importance of the estimate."

We evaluated each population abundance technique with respect to the following considerations: (1) prior and current use of the technique; (2) assumptions (including a list of assumptions for the technique, which of these assumptions can be relaxed and which are critical, and how these assumptions relate to wild turkeys); (3) advantages; (4) disadvantages; (5) design, sample size requirements, and quality control; and (6) cost and manpower requirements.

A long list of disadvantages relative to advantages (Appendix C) need not make a method unacceptable for wild turkeys. Disadvantages and biases can be corrected for in many instances (Overton and Davis 1969:424), and assumptions can sometimes be relaxed. A few strong advantages may outweigh many minor disadvantages, but the reverse is also possible.

Some techniques listed in Table 7.1 and Appendix C have severe limitations, which may explain why they are not used for wild turkeys in the Northeast. *Aerial counts* have rarely been used for turkeys in the Northeast because of the difficulties of observing turkeys in forested habitats. *Line transects* and *strip transects* have seldom been used in this region because of the difficulty of obtaining an adequate sample size with low density populations in forested habitats. Adequate samples would require prohibitively long or numerous transects, and it is difficult to meet the assumption that the animals do not move before they are sighted. *Drive counts* are of limited utility because of the elusive nature and scattered distribution of wild turkeys. The *personal interview-map plot technique* has not been used recently to estimate turkey abundance, probably because of changes in land use and the distributions of suitable participants. The personal interview may be useful for determining distribution, but probably not for estimating abundance. The use of *feeding sites, dusting sites,* or *dropping counts* has been suggested as indices to abundance for wild turkeys, but the ability to locate such signs, and the environmental factors confounding these measures, limit their use for abundance estimation. *Tape-recorded poult distress calls* are useful for estimating brood size and survival of broods of radio-tagged hens. Tape-recorded calls may also be useful to determine distribution, but probably not for abundance estimation. The remaining techniques and tools listed in Appendix C have some potential for abundance estimation, and the following discussions will focus on these methods. Some techniques will be appropriate for a specific research question, but not for management programs, whereas others will be broadly applicable.

Table 7.1. Techniques evaluated for wild turkey abundance estimation

Census techniques
1. Direct winter counts (winter flock/roost counts), including interviewing cooperators
   May be a true census only for the Rio Grande subspecies in Texas; otherwise, an index.

Estimates
2. Aerial counts (may be considered an index, or a subheading of plot/quadrate sampling or transect sampling)
3. Line transects
4. Strip transects
5. Plot sampling (including quadrates)
6. Drive counts (also an index. See Lancia et al. 1994)
7. Mark-recapture
   a. Banding studies
   b. Radiotelemetry
8. Removal methods
   a. Change-in-ratio
   b. Catch-effort
   c. Index manipulation method
9. Map plotting
   a. Personal interview-map plot technique
   b. Map plotting from field observations
10. Double sampling
    For example, combined aerial/ground counts

Indices
11. Brood surveys (may be considered a subheading of roadside counts)
    a. Cooperator brood surveys
    b. Data from field officers/ancillary sightings by department personnel (during routine field duties)
12. Reports from hunters
    a. Deer hunters
    b. Turkey hunters
13. Roadside counts/survey routes
    Includes use of tape-recorded poult distress calls
14. Gobbling counts
15. Track counts (snow track counts may be a subset of, or tool for, direct winter counts)
16. Nuisance/damage complaints
17. Harvest data (related to #8.)
18. Feeding sites
19. Dusting sites
20. Dropping/fecal/pellet counts
21. Frequency indices (may be useful for distribution)
22. Poult survival studies

Tools for the above techniques
23. Radiotelemetry
24. Summer baiting (may be a tool for brood counts, or for capturing birds for mark-recapture)
25. Winter baiting (may be a tool for capturing birds for mark-recapture)
26. Mail-carrier surveys (a tool for roadside counts/brood surveys)
27. Tape-recorded calls (poult calls, male vocalizations)
28. Camera stations (a tool for brood surveys; may be used in conjunction with summer or winter baiting)
29. Adaptive sampling
30. Other sampling schemes
    a. Stratified random
    b. Simple random
    c. Systematic
31. Infrared sensing imagery
32. Hunter check stations
33. Hunter report cards
34. Harvest surveys
    a. Mail
    b. Telephone
35. Field bag checks
36. Agency license/permit sales records
37. Multiple observers
38. Personal interviews/mail surveys of residents or hunters

Chapter 8. Population Census: Direct Winter Counts

Background and Prior Use of the Technique

Stokes and Balph (1965) noted that "accurate inventories of wildlife species clearly depend on a knowledge of behavior. . . . Season of the year and even time of day influence behavior and thus dictate appropriate census methods." Direct winter counts take advantage of the tendency of wild turkeys to form stable winter flocks (Porter 1978), use the same roosting sites repeatedly (Cook 1973), and restrict their movements during periods of heavy snow cover (Hayden 1980). Roost counts have been used primarily with the Rio Grande subspecies, where roosting sites are limited and flocks use traditional roosting areas. Flock counts and various snow tracking techniques have been used across the northern range of the eastern subspecies. Theoretically, once flocks or roost sites are located it is possible to count all turkeys present. If all flocks or roost sites can be located, it may be possible to count the entire population in a given area.

DeArment (1975) used roost counts to estimate the numbers of Rio Grande turkeys in a 2-county area in Texas and calculate the percentage of the population and the percentage of each sex that was harvested. The precision and accuracy of the counts were not evaluated. Roost counts were also examined in Texas by Smith (1975), who attempted to "describe how habitat factors combined with a declining population affected the roosting behavior of Rio Grande turkeys and thus affected roost counts." Cook (1973) examined whether populations of Rio Grande turkeys in Texas could be reliably estimated by interviewing landowners where winter turkey flocks were located. Landowners were asked for roost locations and numbers of turkeys present. Project personnel, assisted by local game-management officers, were also used to locate roosts and to make their own counts for comparison. It should be noted that the Rio Grande subspecies forms socially stable winter flocks and generally uses permanent winter roost sites (Watts and Stokes 1971). Still, many of the concepts can be applied to winter flock counts in other regions where turkeys form flocks and have restricted home ranges, but generally roost at a different site each night.

Little and Varland (1981) used observations of turkey flocks reported by landowners in Iowa to determine minimum population growth and dispersal distance of newly reintroduced populations. Porter (1978) and Porter and Ludwig (1980) used direct counts of all known winter flocks, in conjunction with gobbling counts, to estimate spring population densities in Minnesota. Menzel (1975) obtained information on winter concentrations of turkeys in Nebraska from a mail survey of landowners and observations made by field personnel. Tefft (1996a,b) used flock counts in the *fall*, making use of cooperator sighting reports in conjunction with several other methods, to develop a population estimate in Rhode Island. Weinrich et al. (1985) used cooperators (landowners and other selected individuals such as postal carriers and wildlife agency personnel) in Michigan to obtain counts of turkeys in winter flocks to estimate turkey populations for the purpose of distributing spring hunters by area. Hoffman (1962) used winter flock counts to determine wintering populations in Colorado. Weaver and Bellamy (1989) conducted winter flock counts in Ontario to document turkey population growth from a release 5 years earlier, and have since then been conducting the surveys annually during a 1-week period in March. Lewis and Kelly (1973) performed winter flock counts on a 12-mile² area in Missouri to estimate the population directly between 1964 and 1969.

Assumptions

In using direct winter counts as a census technique, it is assumed that all turkeys aggregate into observable flocks, that flock ranges and flock compositions are stable, and that all flocks can be located. These assumptions may be invalid if some turkeys remain solitary or flock composition and ranges shift during the counting period. In the northern part of the wild turkey's range, "flocks" of as few as 1-3 individuals may be common. Variation in flock size is not a problem if the flock's range is stable. When snow cover is deep, flock ranges will be small regardless of the total number of birds present, so an investigator may be as likely to detect a flock of 1 individual as a flock of 20.

If snow tracks are used to locate flocks, and if abundance data are inferred from the tracks themselves, it must be assumed that the number of tracks correlates with the numbers of birds (Bull 1981). This assumption may not always be valid because accurate track counts are impossible under some snow conditions.

Advantages

In some areas, wild turkeys are concentrated by supplemental feeding or by feeding frequently in harvested fields in winter. As a result, turkeys may be more visible in winter than at other times of the year, making direct counts of individuals easier. Visibility of turkeys is also enhanced because of the lack of vegetative cover in winter (Hurt 1968).

One important advantage of the direct winter count technique, provided the assumptions are met, is that it results in a total count of the population rather than an estimate or index. The method involves censusing an entire area instead of sampling and using statistical manipulations to estimate the population of the entire area (Weinrich et al. 1985). A total count is often easier to explain to the public than estimates based on sampling or indices of relative abundance (Weinrich et al. 1985).

Another advantage of the technique is that it is useful in areas with severe winters because heavy snow cover will restrict the movements of wild turkeys and make them easier to observe (Weinrich et al. 1985). In Indiana, for example, a large percentage of turkeys confined their movements to small areas during periods of heavy snow cover (Wise 1973). The northeastern United States and adjacent Canadian provinces typically experience severe winter weather making this technique potentially useful. Unfortunately, those snowfall conditions that restrict movements of wild turkeys may also interrupt data collection (Hayden 1980). Predictability of snow cover can also be a problem when counts require the participation of many observers.

The cooperation of landowners can facilitate the application of winter counts to areas as large as an entire state. No special sampling skills are required for landowners to count turkeys on their own property, and using landowners minimizes problems associated with agency access to private property (Weinrich et al. 1985). Turkey flocks are rather conspicuous, and they attract attention and interest among residents, which facilitates alerting cooperating landowners to their presence (Hoffman 1962). Cook (1973) compared counts made by biologists with estimates made by landowners of turkeys at winter roosts in Texas and found that landowner estimates "could be used to determine levels and trends of populations where there is little nightly movement from one roost site to another."

Direct winter counts are potentially useful for establishing spring harvest goals. Population estimates based on direct winter counts were correlated with the subsequent spring's harvest in Michigan (Weinrich et al. 1985). In Minnesota, density estimates based on winter flock counts were highly correlated ($r = 0.99$, $P < 0.05$) with spring density estimates based on gobbling counts and observations of the average number of males per group (Porter and Ludwig 1980).

Being able to count the number of animals in a group has the advantage of allowing accurate and repeatable calculations of mean group size (Caughley 1977a:25). Because "the mean size of social groups of gregarious animals tends to increase as density increases . . . group size usually provides a workable index of density" Caughley (1977a:24). Leopold (1944) found this relationship to be true for turkeys, observing winter flock size to increase with density. This measure may also be useful for comparing mean group size among areas or among years, perhaps as an index to food abundance.

Another advantage of direct winter counts is that the method is not labor intensive. This benefit is evident when cooperators are enlisted to collect data. The labor is restricted to the amount of time required to collect the data from the cooperators and process it.

In regions with persistent winter snow cover, flocks can be located by following tracks in the snow. The use of tracks to locate wild turkey flocks or to index populations has been employed by Glover (1948) and Bailey (1973) in West Virginia, and by Eaton et al. (1970) in New York. Plots or transects may be used to find tracks. Following tracks in the snow can provide information on the number and sex of turkeys, their behavior, and habitat use (Healy 1977, Hayden 1980, Burke 1982). Winter sex ratios can provide an index of the potential breeding population and also may serve to give a post-season estimate of the numbers of gobblers harvested relative to hens (Ontario Ministry of Natural Resources 1985). Wunz and Hayden (1975) used snow tracks directly to estimate turkey populations, and found the method reliable in Pennsylvania provided at least 2 days had elapsed since the last snowfall and that snow depth had been >25 cm for at least 2 weeks. Jahn (1973) also noted the advantage of obtaining winter flock counts when deep snow concentrates turkeys.

Disadvantages

Movement of flocks from one location to another can result in inaccurate counts. Midwinter movements were a problem in Minnesota, but flocks did not move extensively after 1 January and few individuals moved between flocks during winter (Porter 1978). Movement of flocks between winter roosts was also a problem in Texas (Cook 1973), and can be a potential problem in any region. Texas landowners often made inaccurate counts of turkeys because of the instability of roost sites and the infrequency of observation (Cook 1973). In many situations observers tend to underestimate the size of large groups (Eberhardt et al. 1979), but Cook found the reverse with turkeys. When landowner estimates were compared with roost counts done by biologists, the landowner estimates were 7-203% greater (Cook 1973). This difference was apparently caused by movement of flocks to different roosts, with subsequent double counting by the landowners. Cook (1973) concluded that roost counts were not a reliable indicator of populations in areas with unstable roost sites.

Smith (1975) also reported that roost counts were not reliable estimators of the winter populations of Rio Grande turkeys in Texas. Roosting patterns were variable and the size of a roost site dictated the size of a flock that could use it. The factors that led to unstable roosting patterns in Texas where turkey densities are low included human activity and land use patterns, relative availability of roost sites, and heightened sensitivity of small flocks to disturbance (Smith 1975). The roosting habits of the Rio Grande subspecies of wild turkey in Texas differ from those of subspecies in other regions. Eastern wild turkeys are usually not limited by the availability of trees for roosting, and they can easily shift to a new roost if disturbed. The problem of flock movement can be minimized by having a short census period (Weinrich et al. 1985), because flocks are less likely to move large distances in a short time. A short census period can also reduce labor costs, especially where biologists are used to conduct the surveys.

In Nebraska, winter counts were not correlated with other survey methods (Menzel 1975). Although Weinrich et al. (1985) found a correlation between winter flock counts and the subsequent spring's harvest, the relationship was affected by sex and age composition, dispersal patterns, land ownership and use, and weather. These factors are potential sources of variation in the use of direct winter counts to estimate wild turkey populations.

The use of landowner cooperators may result in uneven coverage across a study area because the distribution of private land or willing cooperators may be patchy. Weinrich et al. (1985) noted a non-random distribution of wintering turkey flocks in their Michigan study area, associated with private land and the abundance of farming-related waste, storage grains, and supplemental feeding stations found there. However, this concentration of turkeys on private land also made them more visible to the public than if they were on less accessible state or federal land. It may be difficult to find landowners who are willing to participate in the surveys, and cooperator interest in conducting the counts may decline over time (Welsh and Kimmel 1990). Declines in cooperator response rates can lead to underestimates of the turkey population. These problems can be alleviated by using wildlife agency personnel to conduct the surveys, but the cost of such efforts may be prohibitive for large areas.

At present, mean winter flock size cannot be used to estimate population size or index relative abundance. The difficulty with using group size to estimate density in animal populations is that "the regression of density on group size is seldom linear and it usually cuts the vertical axis below the origin; hence the index ranks densities but does not reveal the proportional difference between them" (Caughley 1977a:25). Winter flock size varies within regions (Ontario Ministry of Natural Resources 1985), and apparently responds to many factors in addition to population density (Smith 1975).

The biggest problem with using snow tracks to locate flocks is obtaining suitable tracking conditions. Consistent and persistent snow cover is required, and this condition cannot be guaranteed or predicted in many parts of the wild turkey's range. Bailey (1973)

also found that tracks often could not be located, even when turkeys were known to be present in the general area.

Counts of tracks in the snow are difficult to convert to abundance estimates. An animal can cross a transect or plot many times, obscuring the relationship between numbers of tracks and numbers of birds (Bull 1981). Brower (1990) considered track counts an index of activity rather than a measure of abundance. To use tracks as a density estimate, track counts must be calibrated for animal activity and spatial distribution (Brower 1990:122). Alternatively, tracks can be counted during a brief period following snowfall to eliminate duplicate counting (Wunz and Hayden 1975).

Design, Standardization, and Quality Control

There is no standard method for conducting winter flock counts on wild turkeys, and little methodological discussion of the technique can be found in the literature. The approach used in Ontario by Weaver and Bellamy (1989) might be adapted to other areas of the Northeast:

> The area to be censused was broken up into blocks approximately 4 square miles in area. Landowners and other interested individuals were recruited in each block to observe and report the number of different turkeys seen during a one week period in March. At least two cooperators were used for each block to allow for verification and non-reporting. Whenever possible, the same observers were used for the same block each year. The cooperators were asked to plot all observations on topographic maps to allow for elimination of duplicate observations. Additional blocks and cooperators were added as the turkey range expanded.

Weinrich et al. (1985) used the following methods to count winter flocks in Michigan:

> Counts of winter turkey flocks in northern Lower Michigan were made each January by 6 to 8 people working full time for a period of about 2 weeks. The short census period minimized errors caused by movement of birds between flocks. The census was based on personal contact with observers in turkey range. Census personnel did not actually attempt to count all the turkeys in their area, but utilized networks of contacts which were screened for reliable reports of flock sightings. Initially, the networks were developed from various sources, including newspaper and radio publicity, turkey observation report cards, and observations by postal route carriers, school bus drivers, utility workers, United Parcel Service drivers, and from door-to-door contact with the local residents.

Annual winter flock counts were conducted by the same people whenever possible. Most of these personnel were local technicians, laborers, or part-time employees working under the direction of the district wildlife biologists.

A network of transects that followed ridge lines and drainages were used to estimate winter populations on areas ranging from 81 km^2 to 263 km^2 in north-central Pennsylvania (Hayden and Wunz 1975, Wunz and Hayden 1975). Data collection began after snow depth had exceeded 25 cm for at least 2 weeks, and transects were searched starting 2 days after the last snowfall. Counts were made on foot and with snowmobiles. Tracks were examined to determine number and sex of birds. Data were summarized to determine distribution and minimum number of birds present. The minimum number of birds present was considered a reliable index. Counts could not be conducted in 2 of 12 years because of unsuitable snow conditions (Wunz and Hayden 1975).

Other investigators have made brief comments on their winter count procedures. Smith (1975) made roost counts in Texas at unequal intervals from December through February, in early morning or late evening. DeArment (1975) attempted to calculate an average adjusted population estimate by adding the fall harvest to the late winter population, as determined from winter flock counts. Weaver and Bellamy (1989) conducted counts annually during a 1-week period in March.

Cost and Manpower Requirements

The 1994 cost for the Ontario survey (Weaver and Bellamy 1989) was approximately $1,500 (Canadian), mainly for maps and postage for about 60 cooperators. For the direct winter count done by Weinrich et al. (1985) in Michigan, 6-8 agency personnel were needed full time for a 2-week period. Because cooperators were able to collect all of the field data, the only agency effort required would have been to collect and analyze the data from the cooperators.

Conclusion and Recommendations

Except for specialized circumstances, which include persistent snow cover and restricted flock movements, direct winter counts have limited utility as a census technique (Kurzejeski and Vangilder 1992:176). After considering several techniques for estimating abundance in northern Michigan, Weinrich et al. (1985) concluded that winter counts were more applicable than roost counts (Smith 1975), brood counts (Schultz and McDowell 1957), winter track counts (Bailey 1973), or gobbling counts (Porter and Ludwig 1980) for their area. The Michigan area was characterized by persistent snow cover and agricultural practices and supplemental feeding that caused turkeys to congregate in specific locations.

In regions of the Northeast with persistent snow cover, systematic snow tracking of areas on the order of 5,000-20,000 acres has the potential for providing accurate counts of wild turkeys (Wunz and Hayden 1975). The cost of having biologists conduct the census over larger areas may be prohibitive. The supplemental use of cooperators may result in a reliable *index* of turkey abundance, and provide accurate information on distribution (Weaver and Bellamy 1989). The main problem with the technique in most of the region is that it is impossible to guarantee a continuous series of counts from year to year because weather conditions are not suitable for making counts in some winters. If the goal is to obtain yearly estimates of population size, a method that is less dependent on weather would be preferable. If absolute estimates of population size are not needed for a management program, one of the index methods discussed in the other chapters may be more appropriate for evaluating population trends.

Chapter 9. Population Index: Harvest Data

Background and Prior Use of the Technique

Wildlife agencies commonly use harvest data collected by mandatory checking or mail surveys to obtain turkey population estimates (Kennamer et al. 1992). Table 9.1 shows the types and methods of harvest data collection used in the Northeast. These data can be used to index population trends and densities; index fall hunting mortality rates (DeGraff and Austin 1975, Lewis 1980); or obtain information on hunter satisfaction, attitudes, and field observations (Norman and Steffen 1996). The joint evaluation of fall and spring harvest data can provide information on population trends and the effects of hunting on the population (Steffen and Norman 1996). The most common method of gathering harvest data is mailing surveys to a random sample of permit buyers (Kurzejeski and Vangilder 1992:176). In the Northeast, mandatory check stations are used more often than hunter surveys to monitor turkey harvest.

Several investigators have examined hunting data as a means of estimating or indexing wild turkey populations, or for comparing hunting data with the results of other indices. Palmer et al. (1990) examined hunter success rates relative to population size and found them to be only weakly correlated over a 6-year period in Mississippi. Steffen and Norman (1996) used harvest data from check stations in Virginia to assess the effect of fall hunting on population trends. These investigators, as well as Pack (1993) in West Virginia, found a nonlinear relationship between fall harvest levels and the growth rates of spring gobbler harvests, although fall harvest totals were not related to the size of the subsequent gobbler harvest. In Pennsylvania, the length of the fall either-sex hunting season was inversely related to brood counts in the next year (Wunz and Ross 1990). For Merriam's turkeys in northwestern Nebraska spring hunting success was unrelated to the preceding fall's hunting success or total harvests (Menzel 1975). Porter et al. (1990a) developed an effort-based index to abundance, using the waiting time (number of hunter-days) before the first wild turkey kill of the season in a given town. The reciprocal of this waiting time produces an index that is positively related to turkey density. DeGraff and Austin (1975) used band recoveries from birds harvested in the fall hunting season to calculate the pre-season population size. They acknowledged that banding and band recovery strongly favored hens with broods because adult hens without broods were captured and harvested at lower rates than successful

hens were. Shaw and Smith (1977) used harvest data from both check stations and post-season mail questionnaires in Arizona, and concluded that "the number of turkeys taken by hunters was simply a function of population size." They also found that the percentage of hunters who were successful was directly correlated with the number of turkeys counted during fall roadside surveys. They concluded that the most important factor influencing both success rate and total harvest is the number of turkeys available.

Harvest data can be used to estimate populations with the class of abundance estimating techniques termed *removal methods*. When animals can be readily seen, methods based on observation are generally preferable. For difficult-to-observe species, however, mark-recapture or removal methods are often better choices (Lancia et al. 1994:249). Removal methods are conceptually similar to mark-recapture methods, but "capturing" is done by hunting. Removal has the advantage that it avoids any behavioral response caused by trapping and subsequent release (White et al. 1982), and it avoids some difficult-to-meet assumptions of mark-recapture surveys. Removal violates the assumption of closure, however, and it disrupts the local population, making the method unsuitable for studies to be repeated in the near future (White et al. 1982). This difficulty can be overcome in non-hunting removal studies by marking and releasing captured animals , but not counting these marked animals in subsequent captures (Brower 1990:115-118). The statistics and equations used in some specific removal methods are presented in Brower (1990:115-118).

Classes of Removal Methods

Removal methods include 2 general classes of estimators: *change-in-ratio* estimators and *catch-per-unit-effort* estimators. *Change-in-ratio* estimators "can be used if the proportions of 'types' (e.g., sexes, age classes) of animals in the removals are substantially different from the proportions of the same types in the pre-removal population" (Lancia et al. 1994). This method should be appropriate for spring gobbler seasons, or even for fall either-sex seasons if there is a tendency to selectively harvest certain age and sex classes of birds. The method involves calculating the relative abundance of the 2 types of animals in a population, then removing a known number of 1 type, and then re-estimating the relative abundance of the 2 types, using the resulting change in ratio to calculate the total number of animals in the population (Norton-Griffiths 1978:107, Caughley and Sinclair 1994:208). The method requires surveys, both before and after the removal (Caughley 1977a:38-44, Lancia et al. 1994:250). The change-in-ratio method has been used to estimate the size of pheasant and deer populations, as well as other terrestrial species (see Seber 1982:353), and is frequently used in fisheries studies (Scattergood 1954:280). In one change-in-ratio method, called *Kelker's method* (see Krebs 1989:155), if a population is classifiable into 2 or more classes, such as age or sex, the population size can be estimated after removing a known number of animals from 1 class. Kelker's method is often used to estimate the size of a population prior to hunting that removes mostly males (Caughley 1977a:38-44). This and other methods are described more fully in Caughley (1977a:38-48). Krebs (1989:158) recommends that researchers use the approach outlined by Paulik and Robson (1969) when planning the procedure. Large samples are usually required for change-in-ratio estimators (Krebs 1989:166). Sample size calculations are discussed in Krebs (1989:190-194).

*Catch-per-unit-effort r*emoval models may be used if the removals are not selective, and they have the advantage that "population estimates can be derived from removals that are part of a routine management activity such as hunter harvests" (Lancia et al. 1994:231). The method is only recommended for exploited populations, because it would be too effort-intensive and disruptive otherwise, and is generally less accurate than other methods (Caughley 1977a:17-19). Harvest of wild turkeys is related to the numbers of turkeys present and to the intensity of hunter effort. The catch-per-unit-effort method will presumably eliminate or control the effects on harvest data of changing hunter effort. Like the change-in-ratio methods, the catch-per-unit-effort methods are widely used in commercial fisheries (Seber 1982:569), and have also been used extensively for small mammals. Both methods have been used to develop models for estimating animal abundance. Dupont (1983) developed models for estimating fish populations. Novak et al. (1991) and Laake (1992) modified Dupont's models and applied them to white-tailed deer and elk, respectively. These models have stringent requirements, such as great variation in effort, high harvest rates, and precise measures of harvest (Laake 1992), which may make the models difficult to use in management programs. Williams and Austin (1988) commented that an index incorporating hunting effort was needed to compare gobbler harvest on different areas, and Lint et al. (1995) used harvest per unit effort and numbers of harvested gobblers to derive an estimate that was correlated with Buckland mark-recapture estimates. Glidden (1980) recommended an index based on the number of days of effort per turkey harvested in New York. Gefell (1991) and Porter et al. (1990a), also working in New York, recommended the use of abundance indices based on take and effort on the opening day of the wild turkey season. In all these studies involving wild turkeys, catch-per-unit-effort

indices appeared to be the best of the indices examined to track population trends, but the actual population size was not known.

The catch-per-unit-effort method estimates population sizes based on the decline in catch-per-unit-effort over time. This method requires data on the number of animals removed and statistics indicating effort, such as the number of hunters per unit time or the number of birds seen per unit time. Obtaining data on effort usually requires use of a hunter survey. This method is only appropriate if the removal does not greatly affect the size of the population (Caughley 1977a:17-19). In areas where a substantial proportion of the turkey population is removed, this method may be inappropriate. In these situations, "absolute catch per unit time is a better index" (Caughley 1977a:17-19). Krebs (1989:162), in a seemingly contradictory statement, says that "this method is highly restricted in its use because it will work only if a large enough fraction of the population is removed so that there is a decline in catch per unit effort . . .it will not work if the population is large relative to the removals." Brower (1990:115-118) also indicated that population estimates would be most precise when large proportions of the population have been removed.

Eberhardt (1982), elaborating on a method proposed by Davis (1963), provides another way to use removal data to estimate population size, called the *index-removal method* or *index-manipulation method*. According to Krebs (1989:162), "if an index of population size (like roadside counts) can be made before and after the removal of a known number of individuals, it is possible to use the indices to estimate absolute density . . . Eberhardt (1982) gives the necessary estimation formulas and discusses how this removal method compares with methods based on mark-recapture." Because this method requires 2 surveys in addition to harvest data, it may be too expensive for some management programs. However, harvest data may already be collected as part of the normal monitoring program, and the completion of 2 relatively inexpensive surveys before and after the hunting season may be worth the expense for the quality of data they provide.

Assumptions

A critical assumption for removal methods is that the population is closed (Caughley and Sinclair 1994:208). In many studies, this assumption is violated because "after a few days, individuals originally too far from the grid to have been caught will start moving into the area vacated by the removals (White et al. 1982). Certain catch-per-unit-effort models, however, can be applied to open populations (see Seber 1982:296-352, 541-545 for a full discussion of techniques for these as well as closed-population models). The problem of animal ingress is greater for small grids than for large study areas, because the ratio of perimeter to area decreases as area increases. In the case of wild turkey removal by hunting across a state or large management zone, movements of animals into the study area should be insignificant. Another assumption with removal methods is that aside from the effects of the removal, the population is neither increasing nor decreasing.

The catch-per-unit-effort method also is based on the critical assumption, which should be examined before attempting to use this method, that the probability of capture remains constant. This assumption may be violated because of changes related to weather, food supply, population level, or other factors (Davis and Winstead 1980:233). It is also assumed that catch is proportional to the population and the probability of hunter success depends primarily on population density. This assumption may be violated if factors such as weather or changes in food supply alter hunter success or the population's vulnerability to hunting. It remains to be determined for wild turkeys if there is a threshold above which hunter competence is limiting, which would limit the ability of the technique to track population growth above that threshold, but should not invalidate the index as a warning tool against populations falling below this threshold.

Other assumptions of the catch-per-unit-effort method are that conditions of catching, catching efficiency, and gear are standardized; the removal of one animal does not interfere with the removal of another; and the animals do not learn to avoid capture or become more prone to capture (Caughley 1977a:17-19). It is also assumed that hunter effort and harvest can be measured accurately. This assumption requires that all hunters, including those who were unsuccessful, be included in the sample to obtain an accurate estimation of effort. Seber (1982:296) summarizes the underlying assumption of catch-per-unit-effort methods by emphasizing that the size of a sample removed from the population should be proportional to the effort put into removing the sample. More specifically, "one unit of sampling effort is assumed to catch a fixed proportion of the population, so that if samples are permanently removed, the decline in population size will produce a decline in catch per unit effort."

With change-in-ratio methods, there are 2 critical assumptions (Krebs 1989:155). First, it is assumed that the population is composed of 2 types of organisms, such as males and females, or adults and young. Second, there must be a differential change in the numbers of these 2 types during the observation period (hunting season). It is also assumed that the 2 types of animals have the same probability of removal. Because of sex- and age-related differences in the behavior of wild turkeys, this assumption probably will be violated. Pollock et al. (1985) proposed a method for estimating population size when there is unequal probability of removal. Pollock's method probably would not work for wild turkey harvests because it requires 2 periods of removal, with one class removed in the first period and a second class removed in the next period.

Advantages

The main advantage of using harvest data as a population index is that the data are relatively simple and inexpensive to collect (Stauffer 1993, Lint et al. 1995). Biologists do not need to spend time and manpower conducting censuses, but instead have hunters report the data to them. In some states the necessary information can be collected at hunter check stations. Check stations can provide an accurate count of legally harvested birds at the county or regional level. They also allow the collection of biological data such as age, sex, and weight (Kurzejeski and Vangilder 1992:176). Postal surveys of licensed hunters are also commonly used to collect harvest data.

Lint et al. (1995) showed that harvest per unit effort and number of harvested gobblers were related to mark-recapture population estimates for gobblers in Mississippi. They recommended that these 2 indices be used when examining gobbler population trends, and believed that the number of harvested gobblers "properly indexed gobbler population size." In many states, the data for the harvested-gobblers index are already collected. It may be an easy matter to use *existing* data on hunter effort "to examine possible trends and relations between harvested gobblers and hunter effort" (Lint et al. 1995). Glidden (1980) found that fall harvest in south-central New York was correlated with the pre-season wild turkey population and with hunting pressure.

If the removal is performed by hunters, removal methods may yield more information than mark-recapture (Hanson 1967), but the reverse may be true if hunters are not used to perform the removal (Chapman 1955). An additional advantage is that when removal methods are used in conjunction with an index method, such as roadside surveys, they can be used to estimate absolute density (Krebs 1989:162).

Disadvantages

The greatest difficulty in using harvest data as a population index is meeting the assumption that the proportion of the total population harvested remains constant for the areas or time periods being compared (Lancia et al. 1994:223). Most investigations of harvest rate find evidence of variation over both time and space (Anderson 1975, Clark 1987).

Harvest data from a fall, either-sex season may be difficult to interpret because uncontrollable factors, such as food availability or unseasonable weather, can affect harvest. Years of low natural food availability may force turkeys to forage in open areas such as harvested cornfields, where they are more likely to be seen and shot by hunters, thus increasing harvest rates or harvest per unit effort. Alternatively, abundant natural food supplies may disperse populations, resulting in fewer encounters with hunters and lower harvest rates. Concurrent seasons for other species can also affect turkey harvest. For example, turkey harvest may remain relatively constant over the years even as the population declines, if turkeys are taken incidentally by hunters pursuing other species. Changes in hunter density may also influence hunter success rates (Porter et al. 1990a).

Harvest rate can be standardized by calculating the harvest per unit hunting effort. This measure may not be useful, however, for indexing population abundance when the population size is heavily influenced by harvest. This situation may arise if the population is small, or if hunting pressure is especially intense (Lint et al. 1995), because of liberal hunting seasons or the abundance of hunters. In Mississippi, the relationship between hunter effort and harvest varied between years, perhaps because of changes in gobbler population condition and age structure (Palmer et al. 1990). In New York, traditional harvest-based techniques such as total kill per unit area, change-in-ratio, or catch-per-unit-effort did not produce estimates that met basic tests for accuracy or conformed to normal statistical distributions (Porter et al. 1990a, Gefell 1990). These investigators found no clear relationship between hunter effort and abundance in the following year, and hypothesized that reproduction following the hunting season can offset losses attributable to hunting in the previous year. They therefore used the reciprocal of the waiting time to the first kill of the season as an abundance index, which overcame the problems mentioned for the traditional techniques and provided high precision in their analyses. The relationship among hunter effort, hunter success, and harvest have varied among regions and type of hunting season. Positive correlation between hunter effort and harvest have been reported for New York (DeGraff and Austin 1975) and Florida (Williams and Austin 1988). There was no relationship between total hunter effort and hunter success rate in Florida (Williams and Austin 1988) and Missouri (Lewis 1975). Palmer et al. (1990) observed an inverse correlation between gobbler hunter effort and hunter success rates in a Mississippi population that was declining while hunter effort was increasing.

Another problem with the use of harvest data as an index to population abundance is that hunters may selectively harvest certain age and sex classes (Hanson 1967, Hayden and Wunz 1975, Wunz and Shope 1980). The use of bag checks and wing and leg collections was discontinued in Pennsylvania because the harvest sample was not considered representative of the population (Hayden 1985). Turkeys of certain age classes may be particularly vulnerable to hunting, and differences in behavior between males and females may also lead to a disproportionate harvest of one sex.

The usual goal of obtaining a population estimate or index is to use this information to regulate future hunting seasons. Winter flock counts may provide information necessary to set the following spring season, and summer brood counts may be useful for setting the subsequent fall season. Harvest data are not always helpful for planning future hunting seasons (Wunz and Shope 1980). Data from a fall either-sex hunt, for example, may have little relationship to the subsequent spring's gobblers-only hunt, and little bearing on the population 1 year later before the next fall hunt. For this reason, harvest data are useful for charting trends, but not as valuable as indices or estimates of the preseason population for regulating harvests.

The time and expense required to operate hunter check stations may limit their utility when large numbers of hunters participate and seasons are long. The use of hunter report cards to collect harvest data may greatly decrease agency manpower and costs, but the accuracy of the data may be compromised (Myers 1973). Hunters tend "to inflate their reported hunting success through pride, prestige, or memory loss . . . [causing] large positive biases . . . . Those hunters who bagged nothing are the worst offenders" (Seber 1982:489). Other problems are (1) response rates may differ for successful hunters and unsuccessful hunters, and (2) surveys do not allow collection of some biological data such as bird weights. Furthermore, sample size may be inadequate to provide regional or county information (Kurzejeski and Vangilder 1992:176), making it difficult to calculate variance estimates or otherwise measure data quality. When uncertainty is unknown it is impossible to statistically test data, and the results may only be useful for providing general statements about population trends (Stauffer 1993).

Mail surveys are widely used to eliminate the labor associated with check stations. Mail surveys also have the advantage of providing data from unsuccessful hunters. However, a major problem with the use of mail surveys is that it may take months to obtain names and create a mailing list of licensees. Mail survey data are not available in some states for 12 to 18 months after the close of the season (Kurzejeski and Vangilder 1992:176).This difficulty can be reduced where turkey hunters are required to apply for licenses, because names and addresses of hunters are available immediately. A long delay in getting survey materials to hunters may cause them to forget pertinent details of their hunts (Kurzejeski and Vangilder 1992:176). Connecticut has addressed these problems by including a hunter survey card with every turkey permit and requiring all hunters to complete and return the survey form within 10 days of the close of the season.

Design, Standardization, and Quality Control

Choosing a method of data collection (check stations, report cards, mail surveys) depends largely on the financial and manpower resources available, but is also influenced by tradition and politics. The particular type of data collected is dependent on what type of information the state needs. Hence, it is difficult to recommend standards for harvest data collection.

Table 9.1 lists the methods used and types of data collected in the Northeast.

The basic data required to use removal methods to estimate population size include numbers of birds harvested, hunter effort, and sex and age of harvested birds. Harvest and biological data can be obtained most accurately from mandatory check stations, although report cards and surveys can provide a lesser-quality source of information. Even when hunters are legally required to present harvested birds at check stations, harvest data must be corrected for non-response. Because reporting rates vary among years, periodic corrections for non-response are necessary.

Catch-per-unit-effort methods require the use of surveys to determine hunter effort, with total hours or number of days spent hunting being the usual measures (Table 9.1). Porter et al.'s (1990a) finding that time to first kill of the season can be used to index abundance suggests that date and time of kill should be recorded. In addition to harvest data, change-in-ratio methods require independent estimates of the abundance of turkeys in the harvested age or sex class before and after the hunting season. Check stations and surveys can also be used to collect data on hunter attitudes and experiences, although check stations generally reach only successful hunters.

Cost and Manpower Requirements

The Missouri Department of Conservation compared costs of post-season mail surveys with check stations (Kurzejeski and Vangilder 1992). For mail surveys, the calculation of harvest estimates with 95% confidence limits of ±5% for each county in Missouri would necessitate surveying 99.2% of spring turkey permit buyers. The cost of the survey at 1985 postage rates was approximately $70,450. If the resolution of the survey had been reduced to estimating harvest in the 8 zoogeographic regions of Missouri, the cost would still have exceeded $60,000. To obtain the same reliability level for the fall harvest, an additional $35,000 would be required. These costs do not include data entry and analysis time, so the actual expenses could be greater. The costs of running mandatory spring and fall check stations in Missouri average $40,000 a year. Although the actual costs will vary from state to state, the information from Missouri gives some idea of the relative differences in costs.

Lint et al. (1995) compared the number of harvested gobblers, harvest per unit effort, number of gobblers heard per day, and mark-recapture as indices or estimates of abundance. They found that the number of harvested gobblers was the least expensive, followed by harvest/effort, gobblers heard/day, and mark-recapture.

Conclusion and Recommendations

Harvest data are the easiest and least expensive data to obtain for monitoring program success and population trends. Harvested gobblers and gobbler harvest per unit hunter effort are reliable indices of population trends (Lint et al. 1995). Porter et al.'s (1990a) index to time of first turkey kill in the fall season also provides a useful index to abundance that can be used to monitor trends over time. Because harvest is never perfectly correlated with population size, an independent index of abundance will be required in some management situations.

Harvest data usually need to be corrected for non-reporting bias to obtain an accurate estimate of total harvest. Reporting rates can be estimated with random surveys of permit holders after the season, or by comparing the results from field bag checks with check station and report card returns. Reporting rates need to be estimated periodically because they vary over time. Hunter check stations elicit higher reporting rates than do report cards that successful hunters return by mail. In Missouri, mandatory check stations were less costly than random mail surveys for estimating harvest. Check stations are the preferred method for collecting harvest data in the Northeast.

When the proportion of the population harvested is known from band-return or radio-telemetry data, harvest can be used as an ad hoc estimator of abundance. Harvest data are used to estimate population size in the harvest management models developed in Minnesota (Appendix A) and West Virginia (Appendix B). Mathematically modeled catch-per-unit effort and change-in-ratio estimates of abundance have strict assumptions and data requirements, but they may be useful for research.

We recommend that harvest data collection include date and time of kill, location to the turkey management zone, age, and sex. These data allow calculation of the most useful indices of abundance and provide a complete description of the harvest.

Table 9.1. Types and methods of turkey harvest data collection by eastern states and provinces.[a]

Method	CT	DE	ME	MD	MA	NH	NJ	NY	ONT	PA	RI	VT	VA	WV
Check station	x[b]	x	x	x	x	x	x		x		x	x	x	x
Report card, survey	x		x[c]					x	x	x	x	x	x	
Data collected														
Sex and age	RC[b]	MC	MC	MC	MC	MC	MC	RC	MC		MC	MC	MC	MC
Weight	RC[b]		MC		MC		MC		MC		MC	MC		VQ
Spur length	RC[b]	MC	MC	MC	MC	MC	MC	RC	MC		MC	MC	MS	VQ
Beard length	RC[b]		MC	MC	MC	MC	MC	RC	MC		MC	MC		VQ
Location of kill	RC[b]	MC	MC	MC	MC	MC	MC	MS	MC	RC MS	MC	MC RC	MC	MC VQ
Date of kill	RC[b]	MC	MC	MC	MC	MC	MC	MS	MC	RC MS	MC	MC RC	MC	MC VQ
Hunter characteristics	MS		MS		MS			MS		MS	RC		MS	VQ
Participation or permit use	MS		MS					MS	MS	MS	RC		MS	MS
Hunting area(s)	MS		MS					MS	MS	MS	RC			VQ
Hunting dates	MS		MS					MS						MS VQ
N days spent hunting	MS		MS					MS	MS	MS	RC			VQ
Total hours spent hunting	MS		MS								RC			VQ
N turkeys harvested	MS		MS					MS	MS	RC MS	RC MS			VQ MS
N turkeys seen	MS		MS						MS		RC			VQ
N gobblers heard	MS								MS		RC			VQ
N hens flushed from nests			MS											VQ
Type of hunting implement	MS		MS	MC						MS RC	RC	MC	MC MS	VQ MS
Distance and result of shots fired	MS										RC		MS	MS
N hunters seen	MS		MS					MS			RC		MC MS	
N other hunters interfering													MS	VQ
N hunts disrupted			MS								RC		MS	
Calls, decoys, or guides used			MS							MS	RC		MS	VQ
Illegal activity observed			MS								RC		MS	VQ
Hunter experience level	MS				I					MS	RC			VQ
Time spent preseason scouting											RC		MS	VQ
Amount of money spent	MS								MS	MS	RC			VQ
Hunter attitudes, opinions	MS									MS	RC		MS	VQ
State/federal/private land	MS									RC MS			MC	VQ

[a] Abbreviations:
MC - Mandatory Check
MS - Mail Survey
RC - Report Cards
VQ - Voluntary Questionnaire
x - State uses
I - Incidental/Informal studies.

[b] Connecticut uses mandatory check stations during the fall firearms season. Spring gobbler and fall archery harvests are monitored with kill report cards, and permits for all seasons include a survey form, which must be returned by all hunters within 10 days of the season's closing date. Harvest and biological data are collected with 2 or more methods.

[c] Mandatory survey included with all permits; to be completed by all hunters and returned within 10 days of the season's closing date.

Chapter 10. Population Index: Brood Surveys

Brood surveys have been widely used to obtain indices of abundance or measures of productivity. Field methods varied among studies and the statistics reported include total counts of hens and poults, total number of broods observed, poult-per-hen ratios, mean brood size, and proportion of hens with poults (Kennamer et al. 1975, Menzel 1975, Wunz and Ross 1990). The results of many brood surveys are difficult to interpret because of differences in methods, statistics reported, and the frequent misinterpretation of age ratios. Poult-per-hen ratios alone contain little information about population dynamics (Caughley 1974a). Poult-per-hen ratios do not indicate either the direction or rate of change in a population. Large poult-per-hen ratios can occur with decreasing, stationary, or increasing populations. Age ratios are not adequate substitutes for accurate estimates of relative or absolute density, which are the measures needed for harvest management (Caughley 1974a).

This discussion will be limited to using summer brood surveys to obtain an index to population size prior to fall hunting season. The variable of interest is the total number of hens and poults observed. Other statistics obtained from brood surveys, such as poult-per-hen ratios and mean brood size, are of interest to the observers but are not useful for management decisions. We do not recommend using data from brood surveys to measure productivity.

Assumptions

The basic assumption is that brood counts are related to population size in a constant way. Hens and broods are of most interest during summer because nest success, hen survival, and poult survival are the demographic factors having the greatest effect on population growth (Vangilder and Kurzejeski 1995, Roberts and Porter 1996). Hens with broods are also the most visible segment of the population during summer (Glidden 1980, Wunz and Shope 1980). Brood counts, if conducted in a standardized way, should reflect population size.

We found no formal expression of the assumptions for brood counts and roadside counts in the literature. The relationship between brood counts and population size has not been tested because of the practical impossibility of conducting counts in populations of known size (Weinstein et al. 1995). Population dynamics studies (Vangilder and Kurzejeski 1995) and correlational studies (Wunz and Shope 1980, Wunz and Ross 1990) do support the basic assumption that brood counts reflect population size. In Pennsylvania, total counts of hens and poults are correlated with fall harvest estimated from mail surveys ($r = 0.78$) and hunter report cards ($r = 0.88$), but not with subsequent spring harvest (Wunz and Ross 1990). Similar correlations between brood counts and fall harvest have been found in West Virginia (J.C. Pack, pers. commun.).

It is important to recognize that brood counts have been assessed by comparing them with fall harvest, another index of population size. Fall harvest is influenced by hunter effort, food availability, and weather, so population size is not the only factor influencing the relationship between brood counts and harvest. Despite these extrinsic effects on harvest, brood counts are good predictors of subsequent fall harvest.

Sources of Variation

The most common methods for conducting brood counts are observations by staff and cooperators made during the course of routine field duties, and systematic roadside surveys. Both methods are subject to a number of sources of variation.

Lack of Standardization

Lack of standardization has been a major problem within studies and in comparisons among studies. The problem is greatest when observations are recorded during routine field work, where effort is seldom standardized among years or management units. The general approach has been to include large numbers of observers and assume that variation in effort is randomized across years and management units. Efforts have been made to standardize observer days or miles driven in these surveys with some success. Keeping observers motivated to follow protocol in recording observations is difficult, and changes in staff or field duties can affect the counts. Finally, it is difficult to standardize effort among management units because duties among conservation officers or district biologists vary.

In contrast, formal roadside counts are designed to control effort in terms of numbers of observers, hours of effort, miles driven, time of day, and weather conditions. These surveys are also designed to obtain adequate spatial distribution and comparable samples among management units.

Adequate Sample Size

Obtaining adequate sample sizes has been a problem with both methods. Adequate statewide samples are difficult to obtain with systematic roadside surveys because sampling costs represent a direct expense to agencies. Systematic roadside surveys have generally been applied to specific study areas (Bartush et al. 1985). To obtain adequate samples from observations made during routine field work it has been necessary to extend the observation period through June, July, and August.

Roadside Bias

Roads do not represent a random sampling of the available habitat, and the data from roadside counts cannot be treated like a random sample from a set of transects (Norton-Griffiths 1978, Caughley and Sinclair 1994). These biases have been ignored for statewide surveys where we assume road density and distribution is adequate to give a representative sample of management units.

Observability

Counts of broods are always biased toward underestimation. The observability of poults varies with poult age and habitat type. In good habitat young poults can seldom be seen. Observability increases as poults age, and brood counts tend to increase from June through August (Wunz and Shope 1980). When using total numbers of birds observed as an index to population size, we assume differences in observability due to habitat and age are randomly distributed among years and management units.

Multiple Broods

Multiple broods are often mentioned as a confounding factor in studies attempting to calculate poult-per-hen ratios or mean brood size. Multiple broods do not pose a problem for using total counts of hens and poults to index population size.

Repeat Counts

The issue of repeat observations has not been formally addressed for counts obtained during routine field work. Broods usually cannot be identified individually because birds are not marked, brood size can change, broods move, and counts are often incomplete. Duplicate counting cannot be eliminated because the counts extend over 3 months. Counts can be inflated when an observer reports the same brood from the same place over a period of many days. Such obvious duplicate counts are often deleted, but we know of no formal rules for screening these counts. Repeat counting is assumed to be relatively constant among years and areas for observations made during routine field work.

Repeat counting can be minimized in formal roadside counts by using unique survey routes, or by scheduling runs of the same route over time and controlling for time of day.

Other Approaches

Tape-recorded calls, cameras and bait stations, and mark-resight methods have been used to enhance the efficiency of brood counts or improve the estimates of population size.

Tape-Recorded Poult Distress Calls

Tape-recorded calls have been used to detect many bird species (Stirling and Bendell 1966, Braun et al. 1973, Johnson et al. 1981, Marion et al. 1981). Kimmel and Tzilkowski (1986) evaluated the use of tape-recorded poult calls for locating turkey broods. Only hens with broods responded to the calls, but not all hens with broods came to the calls. Overall, 67% of the radio-tagged hens responded to tape-recorded poult calls, and the response rate of brood hens declined as poults grew older. Tape-recorded calls were effective at luring radio-tagged hens and their broods into areas where poults could be counted accurately. Tape-recorded calls have been useful for getting accurate counts of young broods of radio-tagged hens to estimate poult survival in studies of population dynamics (Vander-Haegen 1987). Tape-recorded calls were not effective in increasing sample size in roadside surveys in Rhode Island (Tefft 1996b). Tape-recorded poult distress calls are a useful research tool, but we do not recommend them for state-wide brood surveys.

Bait Stations and Automated Camera Systems

Bait stations have been used with great success to attract turkeys for capture, and in a variety of ways to detect the presence of turkeys and enhance brood surveys (Speak et al. 1975, Hayden 1985). Monitoring bait stations with automated camera systems holds promise for estimating turkey abundance (Cobb et al. 1996). The efficiency and effectiveness of monitoring bait sites with cameras was compared to standard bait station transect surveys conducted from a vehicle in Florida (Cobb et al. 1996). The camera system produced a much larger sample than the transect surveys (154 vs. 7 observations in 14 days). The camera system revealed that all age and sex classes visited bait sites, and because of the larger number of observations, camera surveys could be completed in 7 days as opposed to 14 days for roadside transect surveys.

The initial purchase of the infrared-activated camera systems was expensive, but these costs can be amortized over several years. Because surveys could be conducted in 7 days (following 7 days prebaiting) camera systems can be moved to sample many areas in one season. The system was clearly effective at indexing abundance on areas of about 3,000 ha; more research is needed to develop the technique for broader application (Cobb et al. 1996).

Design and Standardization

We believe that brood surveys offer the greatest potential for obtaining an estimate of relative density that can be used to regulate fall harvest. Brood surveys have been successfully used for this purpose in Pennsylvania and West Virginia. Based on the available literature we cannot make specific recommendations for conducting these surveys, but we can offer general recommendations for their design.

Observations Made During Routine Field Work
At present, this is probably the most cost-effective approach for state-wide surveys, but the existing models contain a high level of uncontrolled variation. We recommend that these surveys use standardized field procedures and meet specific goals, such as detecting a 10% change at the 80% level of probability. The design should be done in consultation with a biometrician, and should include careful consideration of the geographic sampling units. Once established, sampling design should not be changed unless there is compelling reason to do so. Changing procedures may invalidate comparisons among years. The goal is to produce estimates of relative abundance that are comparable from year to year.

Automate the Tabulation and Analysis Process
This step is important because data come from many observers and results must be available quickly to be applied to fall harvest. Kimmel et al. (1996) described a computerized system for handling turkey observations that included menu-driven database routines and a geographic information system that allowed displaying data as maps or tables. Most states have systems that can accommodate brood survey data.

Consider Enlisting Enthusiastic Amateurs as Volunteers
Volunteers have contributed to the development of large-scale databases such as breeding bird surveys, Christmas bird counts, and numerous state wildlife atlases. Surveys of bowhunters and spring-gobbler hunters can produce detailed and reliable information about many species (Glassock et al. 1997, Igo et al. 1997). Many hunters are skilled observers who spend many hours in the field. National Wild Turkey Federation members are obvious candidates for turkey surveys. Rural mail carriers have been especially helpful (Stauffer 1993), and several states have used mail carriers to obtain abundance estimates of their principal game species (Greeley et al. 1962).

Roadside Surveys
Roadside surveys have generally been carefully designed and have used trained personnel to collect data. One of the most difficult problems is determining an adequate sample size. Several preliminary samples are usually needed to estimate sample size. The model for roadside surveys developed for Florida provides a good example of design considerations (Bartush et al. 1985, Cobb et al. 1996). The Florida system includes bait stations along a 32-km survey route. Criteria are provided for selecting roads, establishing bait stations, and recording data. Surveys are conducted daily over a 2-week period and controlled for time of day, direction of travel, rate of travel, and weather conditions. Details of survey protocol are given in Cobb et al. (1996:217-218).

Chapter 11. Population Index: Reports From Hunters

Wild turkey sightings by hunters have been used to provide an index to population trends, determine distribution, and estimate relative abundance (Welsh and Kimmel 1990, Kimmel et al. 1996). Data on sightings by hunters can be collected by random survey, cards attached to permits, volunteer records, or by interviewing hunters at check stations. Hunter report data for wild turkeys have typically been collected from deer hunters, but can be collected from hunters of any other game, including wild turkeys (Kennamer 1986). Deer hunter surveys have been used most often because they can usually provide large, well-distributed samples. The same data collection procedures will apply to any game survey, although the timing of various game seasons may make certain hunts more useful for predicting subsequent wild turkey harvest.

Background and Prior Use of the Technique

In Minnesota, a random survey of antlerless-deer hunters is used to index yearly trends in wild turkey abundance (Kimmel and Welsh 1987, Welsh and Kimmel 1990, Kimmel et al. 1996). Biologists examined differences in the mean number of turkeys seen per day to detect population changes between geographical areas within a year, and between years within an area. Wild turkey population estimates obtained by wildlife personnel were correlated with number of turkeys seen per hunter per day (TPD), and the percentage of hunters seeing turkeys (HOWT). The HOWT index predicted changes in abundance better than TPD did (Kimmel et al. 1996). The HOWT index had more desirable statistical properties than the TPD index and it was less affected by hunters reporting observing a very large number of turkeys (Kimmel et al. 1996). Hunters may also more reliably remember observing turkeys than recalling the number of turkeys seen. Furthermore, the HOWT index was better than mean TPD scores at reflecting known geographic and annual differences in abundance (Kimmel at al. 1996).

Rolley and Kubisiak (1994) mailed a postage-paid survey form to deer hunter licensees, and evaluated several indices derived from the survey as predictors of turkey population density. They found that the percentage of deer hunters reporting turkey sightings (HOWT) was strongly correlated with the subsequent spring turkey harvest density. They also reported a significant positive correlation between the number of turkeys seen per hunter per day (TPD) and harvest

density. They used a helicopter survey to check the hunter report data, and found that the helicopter survey population density estimates were significantly correlated with the HOWT but not with the TPD index. Deer hunter surveys were used to gather data on turkey distribution in Missouri (Lewis 1980). Both the number of turkeys seen and the percentage of hunters seeing turkeys were correlated with the subsequent spring harvest. The HOWT index had the strongest relationship with spring harvest.

Interviews of successful gun hunters conducted at check stations were used to assess wild turkey populations in Illinois (Garver 1986). The percentage of hunters seeing wild turkeys was more sensitive to changes in turkey numbers than was the number of turkeys seen. The reported locations of turkey sightings were used to determine range expansion. Similarly, Bailey (1973) used interviews with hunters as the most effective means of determining the success of transplanted wild turkeys in West Virginia. Donohoe (1985) used interviews of deer hunters, turkey hunters, and landowners to monitor the distribution and population status of wild turkeys in the Midwest.

Turkey sightings by West Virginia bowhunters are being used to develop an index of abundance that can be used to predict spring harvest (Glasscock et al. 1997). Cooperators, mostly members of the West Virginia Bowhunters Association, maintain detailed records of their hunting activity and wildlife observations during the 6-week fall archery deer season. Examination of the first 2 years of data suggests that turkeys seen per 100 hours may be a better predictor of spring population trends than brood surveys or fall harvest.

Assumptions

The method assumes that the observers are uniformly distributed across the area of interest. Formal models have not been developed for this method.

Advantages

Using hunter reports as an index to wild turkey abundance is cost- and labor-effective, particularly in comparison with route-based surveys (Welsh and Kimmel 1990). Because hunters are already present in the field and require no deployment or compensation by the wildlife management agency, it is a relatively simple matter to collect incidental observation data from them. Other survey methods require expenditures of agency manpower to conduct field surveys, and such surveys can be limited by lack of sufficient numbers of biologists. Because hunters are distributed across an entire state or province, data can be collected over a large area with minimal effort.

Hunters are usually the easiest to identify and most widely distributed group of cooperators an agency can enlist for surveys. It is often possible to sample hunters from specific turkey management units, and data can be collected over a relatively short time period (Welsh and Kimmel 1990). The response rate of hunters remains relatively constant in contrast with landowner cooperator participation, which can decline over time because of lack of interest or other factors (Welsh and Kimmel 1990). The number of hunters is typically consistent from year to year, and hunters may be more inclined to respond to surveys than landowners would be if they perceive that the data will aid in successful management. Alternatively, the submission of sighting reports could be mandatory. Wild turkey sightings by hunters have proven to be an effective index to wild turkey trends (Welsh and Kimmel 1990, Kimmel et al. 1996).

In addition, hunter reports may be one of the most useful tools for determining wild turkey *distribution* and relative abundance (Kimmel et al. 1996). Because hunters may thoroughly cover a jurisdiction, sighting reports may be sufficient to produce a map of wild turkey distribution and relative density across a state or province without requiring the use of agency personnel.

Disadvantages

Obtaining an adequate sample size has been the main disadvantage of random surveys of hunters. In Minnesota, antlerless-deer hunters are sampled because permits are issued for specific management units. Too few permits are issued for some units to obtain an adequate sample. A larger problem was that the sample size needed to detect the desired level of annual change ($\geq 15\%$) for individual TMUs was prohibitively expensive. The problem was overcome by aggregating the 76 permit areas into 15 larger TMUs (Kimmel et al. 1996).

Volunteer cooperator surveys, such as the West Virginia bowhunter and gobbler hunter surveys, provide detailed biological data on many species (Glasscock et al. 1997, Taylor et al. 1998). Inadequate sample size and poor spatial distribution of cooperators are the main disadvantage to these surveys. Indices of abundance can generally be calculated at a regional or statewide level, and little information may be available for some TMUs.

Design, Standardization, and Quality Control

Design and analysis procedures are well developed for random surveys of hunters (Welsh and Kimmel 1990, Kimmel et al. 1996). Methods used in Minnesota to

sample antlerless-deer hunters can be applied directly in states where antlerless-deer permits are issued by management unit. Where permits are not issued for specific management units, the sample can be drawn by location of the hunter's residence. Several indices derived from hunter sightings have been evaluated to determine their statistical properties and relationship to population size. Percentage of hunters seeing turkeys (HOWT) has generally been the most efficient index for monitoring population trends (Lewis 1980, Welsh and Kimmel 1990, Rolley and Kubisiak 1994). Sample size requirements to meet specific levels of precision are discussed by Kimmel et al. (1996). The Minnesota methods have the distinct advantages of automated data processing and mapping capabilities. We recommend using the Minnesota procedures as a model for sampling hunters to obtain sighting data, whether the data are collected from antlerless-deer hunters or another class of hunters.

The other indices and methods for obtaining hunter sighting data have not been as carefully evaluated or standardized. Two other potentially useful methods for collecting hunter observations are used in the Northeast. In Connecticut, postage-paid hunter survey forms are included with all turkey permits: spring gobbler, fall archery, and fall firearms. These surveys have been used to obtain data on hunter attitudes toward regulations, the status of the population, and expenditures for turkey hunting. The surveys always obtain data on dates, locations, and hours per trip; gobblers heard; gobblers seen; hens seen; and birds harvested. Data are summarized annually to produce a variety of statistics including hours hunted per town and hours per kill per town. The Connecticut survey has the great advantages of including the entire turkey hunting population and being completed shortly after season's end. The data can be used to produce a variety of indices of abundance, and the detailed hunter effort could be used for catch-per-unit-effort estimators of population size.

West Virginia enlists volunteer bowhunters and spring gobbler hunters to obtain wildlife sighting data. These surveys produce detailed information about hunter activity, game activity, and observations of many species. The data can be used to produce several indices of abundance. Both methods, mandatory hunter surveys and volunteer sightings, deserve further study and evaluation of the abundance indices.

Cost and Manpower Requirements

In 1995, the Minnesota Department of Natural Resources budgeted about $10,000 for postage and materials for the survey of antlerless-deer hunters used to index turkey abundance (Kimmel et al. 1996). Labor costs are not included, but the survey is conducted from the office by one biologist and no field work is required. The survey cost was estimated to be 63% of the cost of gobbling counts conducted over the same area (Welsh and Kimmel 1990).

Conclusion and Recommendations

Turkey sightings by hunters provide statistically reliable indices of turkey abundance (Kimmel et al. 1996). Sightings obtained by deer hunters after the fall either-sex turkey season are probably the most practical method available for indexing spring population size. Indices based on observations made by fall or spring turkey hunters can be used to validate harvest reports or calculate harvest-per-unit-effort indices of abundance. Surveys used to collect hunter sighting data require minimal labor and expense in comparison with field techniques used to estimate abundance. At present, mail surveys of random samples of deer hunters provide the best method for allocating sampling effort among management units.

Chapter 12. Population Index: Gobbling Counts

Gobbling counts involve recording the number of gobbles and number of individual birds heard from listening stations spaced regularly along transects. Similar call count methods have been used for many upland game bird species. Gobbling counts have been used extensively with wild turkeys for various purposes (Leopold 1944, Dalke et al. 1946, Donohoe and Martinson 1963, Scott and Boeker 1972, Wise 1973, Bevill 1975, Porter 1978, Porter and Ludwig 1980, Hoffman 1990, Palmer et al. 1990, Pack 1993, Lint et al. 1995, Tefft 1996a,b). In the Northeast, gobbling counts have been used in Virginia, West Virginia, Rhode Island, Maine, Massachusetts, and Ontario. Gobbling counts provide 3 types of information: phenology of gobbling, population distribution, and population abundance. Phenology studies have been used to establish the timing of spring season. The success of reintroductions and range expansion of newly introduced populations have frequently been monitored with gobbling counts, and gobbling counts have been used to monitor population trends in many studies.

Assumptions

Gobbling count methods have not received rigorous mathematical treatment and the underlying assumptions have not been explicitly defined. Several assumptions must be made when the gobbling counts are used to index abundance, estimate population size, or determine the phenology of gobbling. First, it is assumed the survey does not influence gobbling activity. If turkey calls or other auditory stimuli are used to elicit gobbling, the data can be used only to determine distribution. Second, it is assumed all observers are equally efficient. This assumption can be tested, or the observers can be screened to meet proficiency standards. Third, gobbling activity is influenced by time of year, time of day, and weather. Gobbler surveys must be standardized to control these sources of variation (Tefft 1996a,b). Fourth, the relationship between gobbling activity and population size is constant. This assumption is common to all index methods, and it is probably only approximated even for specific populations. There is substantial variation among individuals within populations (Hoffman 1990), and gobbling seems to be influenced by the age structure and physical condition of the population (Lint et al. 1995).

Additional assumptions have been made to convert gobbling counts to population estimates. For example, Donohoe and Martinson (1963) estimated the population for their Ohio study area by assuming only adult males gobbled, and adult males made up 25% of the population. In contrast, Bevill (1973) found that 92% of adults and 69% of juveniles gobbled. Porter (1978) derived a density estimate from gobbling count data by assuming juveniles did not gobble, the sex ratio was 50:50, and the age ratio of yearling to adult males was similar to that of females. Because of the uncontrollable variation associated with phenology, weather, and population status, abundance estimates derived from gobbling counts are usually treated as indices.

Advantages

Gobbling is a distinctive vocalization that can be heard for up to a mile under favorable conditions. Gobbling males are easier to detect than hens and juveniles during the breeding season. Gobbling counts do not disturb the population (Bull 1981) and surveys can be conducted in all habitat types (Amman and Ryel 1963). The general location of the gobbler can be determined and fairly accurate locations can be obtained if 2 observers triangulate the direction of the call (Davis and Winstead 1980:224). Gobbler counts are particularly useful for detecting the presence of low-density populations and determining the distribution of flocks prior to the spring hunt (Tefft 1996a,b).

Porter and Ludwig (1980) reported that a combination of extensive and intensive gobbling survey data provided good estimates of relative abundance between years and areas of similar size in Minnesota. The maximum number of groups of gobblers heard in spring, adjusted by the average number of individuals per male group, was significantly correlated with winter flock counts. Gobbling counts were correlated with spring hunter success rates in Minnesota (Porter and Ludwig 1980) and Mississippi (Palmer et al. 1990). Gobbling counts were also significantly correlated with total gobbler harvest in Mississippi (Palmer et al. 1990).

Disadvantages

Gobbling counts are subject to large day-to-day variation (Scott and Boeker 1972, Hoffman 1990), which generally results in weak correlations between gobbling counts and other estimates of abundance (Palmer et al. 1990, Lint et al. 1995). Daily gobbling activity is affected by chronology of breeding activity, gobbler condition, population age and sex ratios, individual variation, and weather; all factors that are difficult or impossible to control with sampling design. Weather affects both gobbling activity and the ability of observers to detect gobbling. Cloud cover, dew, wind velocity, and rain influence gobbling activity (Davis 1971, Bevill 1973), but the relationship among weather variables and gobbling is complex and correction factors have not been developed for these variables. To account for daily variation, gobbling counts are typically conducted on several days each season that meet specific weather criteria. As a result, gobbling counts require a large number of worker-days and a large number of personnel (Wise 1973, Welsh and Kimmel 1990:132). Difference in hearing ability among observers is an important concern (Ammann and Ryel 1963), and conducting counts over large areas creates many logistical problems. Finally, gobbling counts require an adequate road system, and listening points must be free from outside background noises.

Design, Standardization, and Quality Control

Many limitations of the gobbling count technique can be overcome or minimized by standardizing the methodology and carefully designing the survey. Differences in habitat or available resources among agencies may lead to differences in detail, but the general procedure is well established. The technique was summarized in the 1995 report of the Northeast Wild Turkey Technical Committee as follows:

The methods employed in conducting gobbling counts are similar wherever they are used. In gobbling counts, a series of road routes are sampled annually over a period of weeks during the peak of gobbling. This is usually during April and May, but the exact timing varies by year and state. The technique as described by Porter and Ludwig (1980), which is typical, involves survey routes consisting of listening stations at approximately 1 mile intervals along a route 9 to 12 miles long [according to Wise (1973), "gobbler counts were satisfactory when conducted over limited areas so that listeners were no more than 0.5 to 1 mile apart"]. At each stop the observer records for a 4 minute listening period the number of individual birds heard gobbling, the total number of gobbles heard and any noise interference encountered. Routes are run twice weekly from opposite directions starting at 40 minutes before sunrise on days of calm or low winds with no rain or snow. Consistent listening stations along the route are used throughout the period of the survey and from year to year...Scott and Boeker (1972) state that the survey period must include the peak of gobbling activity. They also indicate that due to extreme day to day variation in gobbling activity each route should be run from [at least] three to six times.

Indices produced by gobbling count surveys include (a) the percentage of stops that recorded any gobbling activity for a given year, (b) an activity index equal to the total number of gobblers counted divided by the total number of stops in a given year, and (c) a gobbling intensity equal to the total number of calls counted divided by the number of active gobblers counted (Tefft 1996a,b).

This methodology controls many of the sources of variation in gobbling counts. Details of sampling design are given by Porter and Ludwig (1980) and Tefft (1996a,b). Key design features include standard route length and distance between stations, with permanent reference points for stations. The same routes and stations are used each year. Starting and stopping times, number of times to run route, and direction of travel are specified in advance. Data forms and listening times are standardized, and suitable weather conditions are clearly defined. Artificial calls should not be used to stimulate gobbling, and the observer should not make any unnecessary loud noises.

Ideally, survey dates should correspond with the peak gobbling activity, which may vary from year to year and from region to region. In practice, gobbling surveys are planned to encompass the range of peak gobbling dates for the region, and the maximum counts are used in the analysis. If the peak of gobbling is unknown, a pilot study may be necessary, or information from adjoining jurisdictions may used to estimate peak gobbling dates. Because peak gobbling dates may vary across a state or province, gobbling count survey dates should be specific to a given management unit or physiographic region.

Variability among observers is important and should be controlled. All observers must be thoroughly trained in survey protocol. Standardization of the method with respect to elimination of interfering noises is essential; but, equally trained observers may still differ in their ability to hear calls. This source of error can be minimized by using the same observers every year. Alternatively, the relative hearing abilities of observers can be evaluated by having 2 observers simultaneously run a route and comparing the numbers of gobblers heard by each observer, or by administering a hearing test to each observer before running the survey. It may then be possible to develop a correction factor to standardize the data. The investigator should decide on an acceptable level of precision before conducting the survey, and then replicate the survey, spatially or temporally, to attain this level of precision and to accumulate an acceptable sample size. A pilot study may be desirable to estimate the expected levels of variation and to predict the sample size resulting from a given level of effort.

If the above considerations for quality control or standardization are followed, gobbling counts are potentially useful as an abundance index for wild turkeys. If such standardization is not feasible, or the sources of variability in gobbling activity cannot be adequately controlled, the technique may still be useful for studying the phenology of gobbling and for monitoring distribution. The utility of the technique as an abundance *estimate* is limited by the difficulty in determining the relationship between population size and gobbling activity.

Cost and Manpower Requirements

Welsh and Kimmel (1990) projected that it would require 70 worker-days and a large staff to conduct gobbling counts over a 4,410-km² area in Minnesota. The cost of the gobbling survey led to the development of alternative hunter survey methods to monitor population trends (Welsh and Kimmel 1990). Gobbling counts were conducted on a 14,140-ha area in Mississippi by 2 people working 24 mornings each spring (Lint et al. 1995). In Indiana, gobbling count surveys required a minimum of 6-7 person-hours per bird heard (Backs et al. 1985). Using a combination of intensive and extensive gobbling count methods,

Porter and Ludwig (1980) were able to survey a 2,000-km² area in Minnesota for <100 man-days per year. The 1995 report of the Northeast Wild Turkey Technical Committee described the costs associated with gobbling counts as follows:

Gobbling counts, while not requiring large amounts of overhead, can be labor intensive. Assuming three to four hours for running each route, including travel time, and each route being run four times, the time commitment is about two staff days per route. The number of routes is then determined by variability in counts between routes and desired accuracy of the mean count. The cost could be reduced by using volunteers, but one of the problems identified with the use of gobbling counts is inter-observer variability so great care must be used.

Chapter 13. Population Estimate: Mark-Recapture

The mark-recapture technique involves capturing, marking, and releasing animals, and subsequently recapturing the animals on one or more occasions to determine the proportions of marked animals in the subsequent captures (Bibby et al. 1992:106-107). Captures and recaptures need not be done physically by trapping if the animals can be recognized by some other means, such as wing streamers or radio tagging.

One of the common mark-recapture estimators is the Lincoln-Petersen estimator or the Lincoln "index." The term "index" is misleading because this method produces a population estimate, not an index. This method is the simplest of the mark-recapture methods because it uses a single marking period, followed by a single occasion of recapturing the animals. This estimator is biased upward by birth and immigration, so is best used for populations sampled between birth periods (Caughley 1977a:145).

Because animals are marked only at the initial capture, it may not be possible to mark or sample enough animals to attain reasonably reliable estimates with the Lincoln-Petersen estimator (Eberhardt et al. 1979:9). Methods that employ more than one marking occasion may be preferable, but these methods may increase the time and effort needed to conduct the experiment. The Schnabel method and Schumacher's modifications of this method (Caughley 1977a:145) employ multiple marking occasions, and are somewhat more efficient than the Lincoln-Petersen estimator (Seber 1982:567). Schumacher's method allows a check on the assumption of equal catchability, but the method has more constraints than the Lincoln-Petersen estimator and requires that the population maintain a constant size during the experiment and that no animal dies or leaves the area (Caughley 1977a:145). Several other methods have commonly been used, including the Jolly-Seber method (Jolly 1965) and Bailey's triple catch, which is useful when immigration or birth is occurring, and which gives estimates of birth and death rate as well as population size.

Prior Use of the Technique

The mark-recapture technique has been used with varying degrees of success with wild turkeys and other birds. Everett et al. (1980) used the Schnabel estimator to obtain wild turkey population estimates that were found to agree closely with flock counts conducted during routine field activities. DeYoung and Priebe (1987) evaluated the use of the mark-recapture technique for wild turkeys in Texas, using patagial

tags as the markers. They concluded that the technique may be useful for obtaining population estimates in research studies, but believed the cost and effort required were impractical for management applications. Gribben (1986) evaluated the mark-recapture technique for wild turkeys in Mississippi and concluded that it was too costly and time-consuming to obtain sufficient sample sizes, but suggested that the method may be useful in setting management objectives.

Lint (1990) compared several mark-recapture models for a Mississippi wild turkey population, and found that the Buckland model (Buckland 1980), a modification of the Jolly-Seber model that allows the use off known deaths in the analyses, provided the best estimates of population size. Lint et al. (1995) used the Buckland model to estimate gobbler population sizes for an open population. They compared the Buckland estimate with several harvest-based indices of turkey abundance, and found capture-recapture techniques to be the most expensive. Weinstein et al. (1995) compared 2 mark-recapture models (Jolly-Seber and Buckland) and 2 mark-resight models (Minta and Mangel 1989 and Arneson et al. 1991) with counts made at summer bait sites in Mississippi. They experienced poor performance with both mark-recapture models, probably due to small sample sizes. The mark-resight models performed better, but still produced biased estimates due to violations of assumptions and small sample sizes. They noted that even after large expenditures of money and labor their mark-recapture methods provided inadequate sample sizes.

Bailey and Rinell (1968) used the Lincoln-Petersen estimator, employing band returns, to estimate fall wild turkey populations in West Virginia. Similarly, DeGraff and Austin (1975) used voluntary band recoveries to estimate the proportion of the wild turkey population that was legally harvested each fall in New York. They calculated the pre-season population size by dividing the reported harvest by the direct band recovery rate. An adaptation of this method has been used to estimate spring harvest rates for wild turkeys in Mississippi, where Palmer et al. (1990) calculated harvest rates as the percentage of gobblers tagged January-March that were recovered in the subsequent spring hunting season. They used Buckland's modified Jolly-Seber method to estimate gobbler population size. In Missouri, wild turkeys were captured and marked with patagial wing tags; and data on age and sex ratios, mortality rates, and longevity were obtained from recovery of tags (Lewis

1980). In spite of their sound theoretical basis, mark-recapture techniques have been used infrequently for wild turkeys and other bird species because the techniques are extraordinarily time consuming (Verner 1985:288).

Assumptions

There are 3 general assumptions for all mark-recapture studies (Otis et al. 1978, White et al. 1982) :

1. The population is closed.
Closure refers to the size of the population remaining constant during the sampling period. More generally, closure means that there are no unknown changes to the initial population (Otis et al. 1978, White et al. 1982). In actuality, the population may not need to be completely closed, as long as death and emigration do not occur at different rates between marked and unmarked animals (Eberhardt et al. 1979:7-9). Geographic closure due to physical boundaries is often distinguished from demographic closure that is influenced by birth, death, and emigration (White et al. 1982). Tests for closure are difficult. The assumption is never completely true in natural biological populations and any violation of this assumption biases the various population estimators that have been developed for this technique (White et al. 1982). Models have been developed for open populations, but these methods require more data and more assumptions than closed models require. Open-population models may be useful for conducting long-term population monitoring and for obtaining information on survival and recruitment rates (Otis et al. 1978). The Jolly-Seber model is the most commonly used open population estimator (White et al. 1982:180-187). It allows estimating population size at each of 3 or more sampling occasions and provides estimates of the probabilities of survival and recruitment between sampling occasions. Pollock et al. (1990) believed that Jolly-Seber and related models are preferable to other mark-recapture models, because these estimates are derived from statistical theory. The Jolly-Seber model assumes that all animals in the population have the same probabilities of survival and capture for any one sampling period (Pollock et al. 1990). Pollock (1981) developed a more generalized model that allows different capture and survival probabilities for different age classes.

2. Animals do not lose their marks over the course of the experiment, or the effect of tag loss is corrected in the analysis.
For example, wild turkeys marked with leg bands or wing tags are assumed to retain these tags until their final capture.

3. All marks are correctly noted and recorded at each sampling.
Thus, if turkeys are "recaptured" by remote observation, it is assumed that tagged birds will be correctly identified.

Most mark-recapture models also assume that equal effort is expended on each trapping occasion, and that capturing and marking an animal does not affect its subsequent catchability (Otis et al. 1978:7-18, White et al. 1982). Methods for testing for equal catchability are discussed in Krebs (1989:43-44). Several ways exist that may relax this last assumption (Otis et al. 1978:7-18, Pollock et al. 1990), but the first 3 assumptions are considered essential.

Methods based on analyses of hunting returns have also been developed (Caughley 1977a:157-167, Seber 1982:511-530, Seber 1985). In addition to Assumption 2, these methods also assume that (a) hunting pressure does not steadily increase or decrease over time, although year-to-year fluctuations are allowable; (b) only marks recovered by hunting are included in the analysis; and (c) all ages are equally susceptible to hunting. These assumptions and a set of 7 models used to analyze these types of data are discussed in Caughley (1977a:158-167) and Seber (1982:239-255).

Advantages

The main advantage of the mark-recapture technique is reliability and the sound theoretical basis compared to other abundance estimators or indices. In addition to its utility as a technique for estimating abundance, the method can also provide useful information about other demographic variables (Krebs 1989:15, Pollock et al. 1990, Bibby et al. 1992:105, Caughley and Sinclair 1994:208). The following properties may be examined by mark-recapture experiments: (1) movement, (2) growth rate, (3) age-specific fecundity rates, (4) age-specific mortality rates, (5) size of the population, (6) rate of birth and immigration combined, (7) rate of death and emigration combined, (8) rate of harvesting, and (9) rate of increase (Caughley 1977a:133). Additionally, the method can also be used "to investigate habitat selection and other distributions. . . and to measure reproductive success of individual birds" (Bibby et al. 1992:105). Gribben (1986) also noted the utility of the technique for setting management objectives.

Disadvantages

One of the main problems of the mark-recapture technique is that it is costly, effort-intensive, and time consuming (Caughley 1977a:134, Verner 1985, Gribben 1986, DeYoung and Priebe 1987, Krebs 1989, Weinstein et al. 1995). Another consideration is that "mark-recapture techniques are difficult to use in the real world, and you should be certain they are needed before starting to use these techniques" (Krebs 1989). Davis and Weinstead (1980) provide a list of references demonstrating that mark-recapture methods may underestimate actual population levels considerably.

Mark-recapture methods incorporate several restrictive assumptions that are difficult to meet (DeYoung and Priebe 1987, Krebs 1989:16, Kurzejeski and Vangilder 1992). Indeed, Caughley (1977a:134) concludes that "results are often inaccurate because mark-recapture models are seldom more than a vague approximation to reality," and that the mark-recapture models are not very robust, and "even small deviations from their implicit assumptions can produce large errors in the results." Departures from the assumption of equal probability of capture, in particular, are difficult to detect and may produce biased estimates (Seber 1982:565). Caughley and Sinclair (1994:209-210) believed that mark-recapture methods were of limited utility for wildlife management because the assumption of equal catchability is violated by almost all wildlife populations. In contrast, these methods may be of considerable use in wildlife *research* studies.

The problem of differences in catchability is common among animal studies because age, sex, type and location of traps, type of bait, and environmental conditions can affect catchability. The act of capturing and tagging can greatly alter the probability of recapture of any given animal (Seber 1982:487). For wild turkeys in Texas, DeYoung and Priebe (1987) believed that the assumption of equal probability of capture was not met, because the road network used for the recaptures (resightings in this case) did not uniformly sample the study area. Caughley (1977a:134-139) discusses sources of error due to unequal probability of capture, and presents tests for equal catchability. The problem of unequal catchability potentially can be overcome by using a combined approach employing both closed and open models, as described by Pollock et al. (1990).

Where harvest is used to recover tagged animals, unequal vulnerability to harvest is a problem. Mark-recapture models assume that the probability of shooting an animal of a given age is proportional to the frequency of that age class in the population. This assumption usually is not valid in game bird mortality studies (Caughley 1977a:158). Differences in the behavior of adult versus juvenile wild turkeys lead to disproportionate harvest among the age classes. In this situation, estimates usually need to be made for each age or sex group, leading to greatly increased sample size requirements. If separate data are collected for age or sex groups, however, the method is not appropriate for estimating population structure (Gribben 1986). Non-reporting or mis-reporting of tags from harvested birds may lead to an overestimation of the population size (Seber 1982:489). Because tag returns by hunters are frequently on the order of 30-50%, the marks recovered by hunters can rarely be used to estimate population size (Caughley 1977a:157). Generally, only mortality rates can be calculated from mark-recapture experiments using hunting returns.

A related problem is that different types of tags have different recovery or retention rates on wild turkeys (Myers 1973). Thus, fewer birds may be counted as recaptures than would be the case if all tags were retained, leading to biased or non-comparable data. Caughley (1977a:139) points out that few systems for marking animals are permanent (particularly bird bands), and he also discusses testing for loss of marks.

Obtaining a sufficient sample size may restrict the use of the mark-recapture technique because a large proportion of the population needs to be marked for adequate accuracy. Several investigators have suggested marking at least 50% of the population for Lincoln-Petersen estimates (Caughley 1977a, Seber 1982, Krebs 1989). For wild turkey populations occupying areas of more than a few thousand acres, such a sample size may be unattainable. Capture of turkeys is often too difficult to provide adequate sample sizes for population studies (Gribben 1986).

Skalski and Robson (1992) noted that mark-recapture methods typically serve to estimate abundance at a single plot, which means that statistical inference is limited to abundance of the animals in that study area, rather than for the overall contiguous population or the mean abundance of the overall area. Caughley (1977a:140) similarly noted that in attempting to interpret population size by mark-recapture, the population often has no distinct boundary, and therefore limits the estimation to a study area of arbitrary size. Lint et al. (1992) discussed the problems of using arbitrary study area boundaries to derive population and density estimates for wild turkeys and described a method for estimating effective study area size from tag-returns of marked and harvested wild turkeys. Thus, if a mark-recapture study were conducted in a local study area, the extension of the results to the entire management area would be unjustified.

Design, Standardization, and Quality Control

The methodology for mark-recapture field techniques and statistical analyses is well developed. The selection of a particular mark-recapture estimator depends on the assumptions that can be made about the population and the procedure (Eberhardt et al. 1979:7). We cannot recommend a single best protocol for use with any wild turkey population, because the assumptions need to be evaluated for each population before a method can be selected. The mark-recapture method should always be selected *before* attempting to collect field data, and testing of the assumptions should be incorporated into the sampling program (Krebs 1989:59-60). The investigator who wants to employ mark-recapture methods should first consult the pertinent literature.

Krebs (1989:59-60) and Lancia et al. (1994 239-247) summarize the various methods used to analyze mark-recapture data. A comprehensive synthesis of the wildlife and statistical literature on mark-recapture studies can be found in Cormack (1968) and Otis et al. (1978). Seber (1973) is an earlier but useful review summarizing the existing literature on this method to that date. Seber (1982) incorporates more recent developments, and gives an excellent discussion of the Jolly-Seber and other mark-recapture models. He also discusses in detail departures from the various assumptions, and statistical tests to determine whether these departures are significant. White et al.

(1982) provides a follow-up to Otis et al. (1978), providing a comprehensive primer on closed-population mark-recapture methods including references on field procedures. White et al. (1978) provide a computer program (CAPTURE) to carry out the calculations, along with a commentary on the use of the program. Verner (1985:288) commented that this program "is an essential tool for anyone using capture-recapture methods that assume a closed population." CAPTURE, however, "does not perform well when capture probabilities are small and population sizes are small" (Pollock et al. 1990). Pollock et al. (1990) present methodology to design, analyze, and conduct long-term mark-recapture experiments, and present new material that was not previously discussed by Seber (1982). They discuss several variations of the Jolly-Seber model for open populations, and present 2 computer programs for the analysis of mark-recapture data (JOLLY and JOLLYAGE). A recent program, NOREMARK, which produces 4 estimators of population abundance, was presented by White (1996) for situations such as radiotelemetry studies where animals are initially marked but are only observed, rather than recaptured, in subsequent samples.

The critical assumption of closure can be met or approximated by timing the sampling periods to avoid times of migration or recruitment, and by running the experiment over as short a period of time as possible (White et al. 1982:162). If there is no way to ensure that the population size is not undergoing change during the period of the investigation, an open-population model should be used. The problem with open models, however, is that these methods require more data than closed models do because assumptions are more rigorous and more parameters are involved (Otis et al. 1978:7-18).

Skalski and Robson (1992:58) recommend that unless prior estimates of population parameters are available and reliable, preliminary surveys should be considered as the first step in most field investigations that will use capture data to make inference to population effect. They also provide recommendations for the design and analysis of these preliminary surveys.

Cost and Manpower Requirements

Buckland et al. (1993) lists several references indicating that mark-recapture techniques are relatively expensive compared to line transects. One such comparison was performed for bobwhite by Shupe et al. (1987), who used a helicopter to count birds along transects. They found that mark-recapture estimates were more expensive than the aerial transects, which in turn were more expensive than drive counts. They also noted that mark-recapture methods were 3 times more expensive than ground-based (walking) line transects in rangeland studies in Texas. Thus, mark-recapture was the most expensive of the 4 methods examined. DeYoung and Priebe (1987) evaluated mark-recapture techniques for wild turkeys in Texas and concluded that the required cost

and effort made the technique impractical for large-area management uses. Similarly, Gribben (1986), who evaluated the mark-recapture technique for wild turkeys in Mississippi, concluded that the technique is costly and time consuming, but may be of some use in setting management objectives. Lint et al. (1995) compared various methods of indexing or estimating wild turkey gobbler abundance and ranked 4 methods in order of decreasing cost as (a) mark-recapture, (b) number of gobblers heard per day, (c) harvest per unit effort, and (d) number of harvested gobblers. In contrast, Guthery (1988) examined bobwhite density on rangeland and found that labor required for the Lincoln-Petersen mark-recapture method was comparable to that for the line transect method. Compared with change-in-ratio removal methods, the Lincoln-Petersen method has been claimed to be "better value for the money" (Seber 1982). Skalski and Robson (1992) discuss the calculation of costs associated with trapping studies.

Conclusion and Recommendations

The mark-recapture technique will be most useful as a research tool for studying population dynamics, or for calibrating and validating population indices obtained with other techniques. The technique will be useful mainly in intensive studies, as opposed to statewide or provincial management applications. In research situations where the technique is feasible, it can provide reliable estimates of absolute abundance and other demographic variables. In Seber's (1982:564) comprehensive book discussing the main methods for estimating or indexing animal abundance, he concludes that "of all the methods considered in this book, the [Lincoln-Petersen] method appears to be the most useful, provided that the assumptions underlying the method are satisfied and there are sufficient recaptures in the second sample." Compared with removal methods, populations can be sampled more reliably and efficiently using mark-recapture techniques (Pollock and Kendall 1987). Otis et al. (1978:67) and White et al. (1982:162) recommend the use of live trapping (mark-recapture) studies over removal methods because of the "wider array of options available for the data analysis." In addition, removal methods disrupt the population, which may lead to immigration when large numbers of animals are removed, thus violating the assumption of closure.

The mark-recapture technique is not useful for routine long-term monitoring applications because of the costs associated with capturing adequate numbers of birds and the difficulty of observing marked birds (Kurzejeski and Vangilder 1992). Estimates of absolute abundance are seldom necessary for harvest management, and population trends can generally be monitored with indices of abundance. Intensive population studies involving large numbers of marked birds offer opportunities for employing mark-recapture methods to validate other, less costly indices of abundance (Lint et al. 1995).

Literature Cited

Aldrich, J. W. 1967. Historical background. Pages 6-16 *in* O. H. Hewitt, ed. The wild turkey and its management. The Wildlife Society, Washington, D. C.

Ammann, G. A., and L. A. Ryel. 1963. Extensive methods in inventorying ruffed grouse in Michigan. J. Wildl. Manage. 27:617-633.

Anderson, D. R. 1975. Population ecology of the mallard. V. Temporal and geographic estimates of survival, recovery, and harvest rates. U.S. Fish and Wildl. Serv. Resour. Publ. 125. 110 pp.

Anderson, D. R., J. L. Laake, B. R. Crain, and K. P. Burnham. 1979. Guidelines for line transect sampling of biological populations. J. Wildl. Manage. 43:70-78.

Applegate, R. D. 1997. A rural mail carrier survey index for Kansas wild turkeys. Trans. Kansas Acad. Sci. 100:80-84.

Arneson, A. N., C. J. Schwarg, and J. M. Gerrard. 1991. Estimating closed population size and number of marked animals from sighting data. J. Wildl. Manage. 55:716-730.

Audubon, J. J. 1967. The birds of America. Dover Publications, Inc., New York.

Backs, S. E., R. P. Bouta, and R. M. Platte. 1985. Use of landowner and resident observations to evaluate wild turkey releases. Proc. National Wild Turkey Symposium 5:259-268.

Bailey, R. W. 1956. Sex determination of adult wild turkeys by means of dropping configuration. J. Wildl. Manage. 20:220.

Bailey, R. W. 1973. Restoring wild-trapped turkeys to nonprimary range in West Virginia. Pages 181-185 *in* G. C. Sanderson and H. C. Schultz, eds. Wild turkey management: current problems and programs. Missouri Chapter of The Wildlife Society and University of Missouri Press, Columbia.

Bailey, R. W. 1980. The wild turkey status and outlook in 1979. Proc. National Wild Turkey Symposium 4:1-9.

Bailey, R. W., and K. T. Rinell. 1967. Events in the turkey year. Pages 73-91 *in* O.H. Hewitt, ed. The wild turkey and its management. The Wildlife Society, Washington, D.C.

Bailey, R. W., and K. T. Rinell. 1968. History and management of the wild turkey in West Virginia. West Virginia Division of Game and Fish, Charleston. 59 pp.

Bartush, W. S., M. S. Sasser, and D. L. Francis. 1985. A standardized turkey brood survey method for northwest Florida. Proc. National Wild Turkey Symposium 5:173-181

Beasom, S. L. 1970. Productivity of bearded wild turkey hens in south Texas. J. Wildl. Manage. 34:183-186.

Beasom, S. L. 1973. Ecological factors affecting wild turkey reproductive success in south Texas. Ph.D. Diss., Texas A & M Univ. 215 pp.

Beasom, S. L., and O. H. Pattee. 1980. The effect of selected climatic variables on wild turkey productivity. Proc. National Wild Turkey Symposium 4:127-135.

Bevill, W. V., Jr. 1973. Some factors influencing gobbling activity among wild turkeys. Proc. Annu. Conf. Southeast. Assoc. Game and Fish Comm. 27:62-73.

Bevill, W. V. 1975. Setting spring gobbler hunting seasons by timing peak gobbling. Proc. National Wild Turkey Symposium 3:198-204.

Bibby, C. J., N. D. Burgess, and D. A. Hill. 1992. Bird census techniques. Academic Press Inc., San Diego, Calif.

Braun, C. L., R. K. J. Schmidt, and G. E. Rogers. 1973. Census of Colorado white-tailed ptarmigan with tape-recorded calls. J. Wildl. Manage. 37:90-93.

Brower, J. E. 1990. Field and laboratory methods for general ecology. Wm. C. Brown Publishers, Dubuque, Iowa.

Buckland, S. T. 1980. A modified analysis of the Jolly-Seber capture-recapture model. Biometrics 36:419-435.

Buckland, S. T., D. R. Anderson, K. P. Burnham, and J. L. Laake. 1993. Distance sampling: estimating abundance of animal populations. Chapman and Hall, London.

Bull, E. L. 1981. Indirect estimates of abundance of birds. Pages 76-80 *in* C. J. Ralph and J. M. Scott, eds. Estimating numbers of terrestrial birds. Studies in Avian Biology No. 6. Cooper Ornithological Society, Los Angeles.

Burke, C. J. 1982. Wisconsin turkey hunter's guide. Lacrosse, Wis.

Burnham, K. P., and D. R. Anderson. 1984. The need for distance data in aerial counts. J. Wildl. Manage. 48:1248-1254.

Burnham, K. P., D. R. Anderson, and J. L. Laake. 1980. Estimation of density from line transect sampling of biological populations. Wildl. Monogr. 72:1-202.

Burnham, K. P., D. R. Anderson, and J. L. Laake. 1985. Efficiency and bias in strip and line transect sampling. J. Wildl. Manage. 49:1012-1018.

Cardoza, J. E. 1995. A possible longevity record for the wild turkey. J. Field Ornithology 66:267-269.

Caughley, G. 1974a. Interpretation of age ratios. J. Wildl. Manage. 38:557-562.

Caughley, G. 1974b. Bias in aerial survey. J. Wildl. Manage. 38:921-933.

Caughley, G. 1977a. Analysis of vertebrate populations. 1980 reprint, with corrections. John Wiley & Sons, New York.

Caughley, G. 1977b. Sampling in aerial survey. J. Wildl. Manage. 41:605-615.

Caughley, G. 1985. Harvesting of wildlife: past, present and future. Pages 3-14 in S. L. Beasom and S. F. Roberson, eds. Game harvest management. Caesar Kleberg Wildlife Research Institute, Kingsville, Texas.

Caughley, G., and J. Goddard. 1972. Improving the estimates from inaccurate censuses. J. Wildl. Manage. 36:135-140.

Caughley, G., and A. R. E. Sinclair. 1994. Wildlife ecology and management. Blackwell Science, Inc., Cambridge, Mass.

Caughley, G., R. Sinclair, and D. Scott-Kemmis. 1976. Experiments in aerial survey. J. Wildl. Manage. 40:290-300.

Chapman, D. G. 1955. Population estimation based on change of composition caused by a selective removal. Biometrika 42:279-290.

Clark, W. R. 1987. Effects of harvest on annual survival of muskrats. J. Wildl. Manage. 51:265-272.

Cobb, D. T., D. L. Francis, and R. W. Etters. 1996. Validating a wild turkey population survey using cameras and infrared sensors. Proc. National Wild Turkey Symposium 7:213-218.

Cochran, W. G. 1977. Sampling techniques. John Wiley & Sons, Inc., New York.

Cook, R. L. 1973. A census technique for the Rio Grande turkey. Pages 279-283 in G. C. Sanderson and H. C. Schultz, eds. Wild turkey management: current problems and programs. Missouri Chapter of The Wildlife Society and University of Missouri Press, Columbia.

Cormack, R. M. 1968. The statistics of capture-recapture methods. Oceanogr. Mar. Biol. Annu. Rev. 6:455-506.

Craig, R., and H. Suetsugu. 1973. Surveys and management of wild turkey. Nebraska Game and Parks Comm. 14 pp.

Dalke, P. A., A. S. Leopold, and D. L. Spencer. 1946. The ecology and management of the wild turkey in Missouri. Missouri Conservation Comm. Tech. Bull. No.1., 86 pp.

Davis, D. E. 1963. Estimating the numbers of game populations. Pages 89-118 in H. S. Mosby, ed. Wildlife investigational techniques. The Wildlife Society, Washington, D.C.

Davis, D. E., and R. L. Winstead. 1980. Estimating the numbers of wildlife populations. Pages 221-245 in S. D. Schemnitz, ed. Wildlife management techniques manual. The Wildlife Society, Washington, D.C.

Davis, J. R. 1971. Spring weather and wild turkeys. Ala. Conserv. 41:6-7.

DeArment, R. D. 1975. Either-sex turkey harvest in the Texas panhandle. Proc. National Wild Turkey Symposium 3:189-190.

DeGraff, L. W., and D. E. Austin. 1975. Turkey harvest management in New York. Proc. National Wild Turkey Symposium 3:191-197.

DeYoung, C. A., and J. C. Priebe. 1987. Comparison of inventory methods for wild turkeys in south Texas. Proc. Annu. Conf. Southeast. Assoc. Fish Wildl. Agencies 41:294-298.

Dice, L. R. 1938. Some census methods for mammals. J. Wild. Manage. 2:119-130.

Dickson, J. G., ed. 1992. The wild turkey: biology and management. Stackpole Books, Harrisburg, Pa.

Donohoe, R. W. 1985. Distribution and population status of midwestern wild turkeys, spring 1983. Proc. National Wild Turkey Symposium 5:303-308.

Donohoe, R. W., and R. K. Martinson. 1963. Wild turkey inventory, 1958-61. Game Research in Ohio. 2:43-45.

Donohoe, R. W., W. P. Parker, M. W. McClain, and C. E. McKibben. 1983. Distribution and population estimates of Ohio wild turkeys (Meleagris gallopavo), 1981-82. Ohio J. Sci. 83:188-190.

Dupont, W. D. 1983. A stochastic catch-effort method of estimating animal abundance. Biometrics 39:1021-1033.

Eaton, S. W., T. L. Moore, and E. N. Saylor. 1970. A ten year study of the food habits of a northern population of wild turkeys. Sci. Stud. 26:43-64.

Eberhardt, L. L. 1978a. Appraising variability in population studies. J. Wildl. Manage. 42:207-238.

Eberhardt, L. L. 1978b. Transect methods for population studies. J. Wildl. Manage. 42:1-31.

Eberhardt, L. L. 1982. Calibrating an index by using removal data. J. Wildl. Manage. 46:734-740.

Eberhardt, L. L., D. G. Chapman, and J. R. Gilbert. 1979. A review of marine mammal census methods. Wildl. Monogr. 63:1-46.

Eberhardt, L. L., and M. A. Simmons. 1987. Calibrating population indices by double sampling. J. Wildl. Manage. 51:665-675.

Everett, D., D. W. Speake, and K. Maddox. 1980. Natality and mortality of a north Alabama wild turkey population Proc. National Wild Turkey Symposium 4:117-125.

Exum, J. H., J. A. McGlincy, D. W. Speake, J. L. Buckner, and F. M. Stanley. 1987. Ecology of the eastern wild turkey in an intensively managed pine forest in southern Alabama. Bull. Tall Timbers Research Station 23:1-70.

Gardner, D. T., D. W. Speake, and W. J. Fleming. 1973. The effects of a spring "gobbler-only" hunting season on wild turkey reproduction and population size. Proc. Annu. Conf. Southeast. Assoc. Game and Fish Comm. 26:244-252.

Garver, J. K. 1986. Population studies of wild turkeys: cooperative landowner turkey brood survey and deer hunter survey. Illinois Forest Game Program. Annual Report. 14 pp.

Gefell, D. J. 1990. Extrinsic influences on population dynamics of wild turkeys in New York. M.S. Thesis. State Univ. New York, College of Environmental Science and Forestry, Syracuse. 180 pp.

Gefell, D. J. 1991. An exploration of the influence of environmental factors on variation in wild turkey populations. Ph.D. Diss. State Univ. New York, College of Environmental Science and Forestry, Syracuse. 215 pp.

Getz, W. M., and R. G. Haight. 1989. Population harvesting: demographic models of fish, forest, and animal resources. Princeton University Press, Princeton, N. J.

Glasscock, A. C., J. M. Crumb, J. C. Pack, and R. L. Tucker. 1997. 1996 West Virginia bowhunter survey. West Virginia Division of Natural Resources, Petersburg. 28 pp.

Glidden, J. W. 1980. An examination of fall wild turkey hunting statistics from different ecological areas of southwestern New York. Proc. National Wild Turkey Symposium 4:76-85.

Glidden, J. W., and D. E. Austin. 1975. Natality and mortality of wild turkey poults in southwestern New York. Proc. National Wild Turkey Symposium 3:48-54.

Glover, F. A. 1948. Winter activities of wild turkey in West Virginia. J. Wildl. Manage. 12:416-427.

Greeley, F., R. F. Labisky, and S. H. Mann. 1962. Distribution and abundance of pheasants in Illinois. Illinois Natural History Survey, Urbana, Bull. Biol. Notes. 16 pp.

Gribben, K. J. 1986. Population estimates for the wild turkey in east-central Mississippi. M.S. Thesis. Mississippi State Univ., Mississippi State. 95 pp.

Guthery, F. S. 1988. Line transect sampling of bobwhite density on rangeland: evaluation and recommendations. Wildl. Soc. Bull. 16:193-203.

Hanson, W. R. 1967. Estimating the density of an animal population. J. Res. Lepid. 6:203-247.

Hayden, A. H. 1980. Dispersal and movements of wild turkeys in northern Pennsylvania. Trans. Northeast Sect. Wildl. Soc. 37:258-265.

Hayden, A. H. 1985. Summer baiting as an indicator of wild turkey population trends and harvest. Proc. National Wild Turkey Symposium 5:245-252.

Hayden, A. H., and G. A. Wunz. 1975. Wild turkey population characteristics in northern Pennsylvania. Proc. National Wild Turkey Symposium 3:131-140.

Healy, W. M. 1977. Wild turkey winter habitat in West Virginia cherry-maple forests. Trans. Northeast Fish and Wildl. Conf. 34:7-12.

Healy, W. M. 1997. Thinning New England oak stands to enhance acorn production. Northern J. Applied Forestry 14:152-156.

Healy, W. M., and E. S. Nenno. 1985. Effect of weather on wild turkey poult survival. Proc. National Wild Turkey Symposium 5:91-101.

Healy, W. M., A. M. Lewis, and E. F. Boose. 1999. Variation of red oak acorn production. Forest Ecology and Management 116:1-11.

Hewitt, O. H., ed. 1967a. The wild turkey and its management. The Wildlife Society, Washington, D. C.

Hewitt, O. H. 1967b. A road-count index to breeding populations of red-winged blackbirds. J. Wildl. Manage. 31:39-49.

Hoffman, D. M. 1962. The wild turkey in eastern Colorado. Colorado Game and Fish Department. Tech. Publ. No. 12. 47 pp.

Hoffman, R. W. 1990. Chronology of gobbling and nesting activities of Merriam's wild turkeys. Proc. National Wild Turkey Symposium 6:25-31.

Hoskinson, R. L. 1976. The effect of different pilots on aerial telemetry error. J. Wildl. Manage. 40:137-139.

Howell, J. C. 1951. The roadside census as a census method of measuring bird populations. Auk 68:334-357.

Hubbard, M. W., D. L. Garner, and E. E. Klaas. 1999. Wild turkey poult survival in southcentral Iowa. J. Wildl. Manage. 63:199-203.

Hurt, J. J. 1968. Surveys and management of wild turkeys. Nebraska Game and Parks Comm. Pittman-Robertson Report W-15-R-24. 18 pp.

Igo, W. K., C. I. Taylor, G. H. Sharp, J. E. Evans, R. L. Tucker, and J. C. Pack. 1997. 1996 spring gobbler survey. West Virginia Division of Natural Resources, Wildlife Resources Section, Elkins. 20pp.

Jahn, L. R. 1973. Summary: needs and opportunities for managing turkey populations. Pages 317-324 in G. C. Sanderson and H. C. Schultz, eds. Wild turkey management: current problems and programs. Missouri Chapter of The Wildlife Society and University of Missouri Press, Columbia.

Järvinen, O. 1976. Estimating relative densities of breeding birds by the line transect method. II. Comparison between two methods. Ornis Scand. 7:43-48.

Johnson, R. R., B. T. Brown, L. T. Haight, and J. M. Simpson. 1981. Playback recordings as a special avian censusing technique. Pages 68-75 in C. J. Ralph and J. M. Scott, eds. Estimating numbers of terrestrial birds. Studies in Avian Biology No. 6. Cooper Ornithological Society, Los Angeles.

Jolly, G. M. 1965. Explicit estimates from capture-recapture data with both death and immigration-stochastic model. Biometrika 52:225-247.

Keegan, T. W., and J. A. Crawford. 1999. Reproduction and survival of Rio Grande turkeys in Oregon. J. Wildl. Manage. 63:204-210.

Kennamer, J. E., ed. 1986. Guide to the American wild turkey. National Wild Turkey Federation, Edgefield, S.C. 189 pp.

Kennamer, J. E., D. H. Arner, C. R. Hopkins, and R. C. Clanton. 1975. Productivity of the eastern wild turkey in the Mississippi Delta. Proc. National Wild Turkey Symposium 3:41-47.

Kennamer, M. C., R. E. Brenneman, and J. E. Kennamer. 1992. Guide to the American wild turkey, part 1: status-numbers, distribution, seasons, harvests and regulations. National Wild Turkey Federation, Edgefield, S.C.

Kienzler, J. M., T. W. Little, and W. A. Fuller. 1996. Effects of weather, incubation, and hunting on gobbling activity in wild turkeys. Proc. National Wild Turkey Symposium 7:61-67.

Kimmel, R. O., J. H. Poate, and M. R. Riggs. 1996. Spatial handling of wild turkey survey data using geographic information system mapping procedures. Proc. National Wild Turkey Symposium 7:219-223.

Kimmel, R. O., and R. J. Welsh. 1987. Wild turkey sightings by antlerless deer hunters: an index to Minnesota's wild turkey population. Pages 14-17 in B. Joselyn, ed. Summaries of wildlife research project findings, 1986-1987. Minnesota Department of Natural Resources, St. Paul.

Kimmel, V. L., and W. M. Tzilkowski. 1986. Eastern wild turkey responses to a tape-recorded chick call. Wildl. Soc. Bull. 14:55-59.

Koenig, W. D., R. L. Mumme, W. J. Carmen, and M. T. Stanback. 1994. Acorn production by oaks in central coastal California: variation within and among years. Ecology 75:99-109.

Krebs, C. J. 1985. Ecology: the experimental analysis of distribution and abundance. Harper and Row, Publishers, New York.

Krebs, C. J. 1989. Ecological methodology. Harper and Row, Publishers, New York.

Kurzejeski, E. W., and J. B. Lewis. 1990. Home ranges, movements, and habitat use of wild turkey hens in northern missouri. Proc. National Wild Turkey Symposium 6:67-71.

Kurzejeski, E. W., and L. D. Vangilder. 1992. Population management. Pages 165-185 in J. G. Dickson, ed. The wild turkey: biology and management. Stackpole Books, Harrisburg, Pa.

Laake, J. L. 1992. Catch effort models and their application to elk in Colorado. Ph.D. Diss. Colorado State University, Ft. Collins. 116 pp.

Lancia, R. A., J. D. Nichols, and K. H. Pollock. 1994. Estimating the numbers of animals in wildlife populations. Pages 215-253 in T. A. Bookhout, ed. Research and management techniques for wildlife and habitats. The Wildlife Society, Bethesda, Md.

Leopold, A. S. 1944. The nature of heritable wildness in turkeys. Condor 46:133-197.

LeResche, R. E., and R. A. Rausch. 1974. Accuracy and precision of aerial moose censusing. J. Wildl. Manage. 38:175-182.

Lewis, J. B. 1975. Evaluation of spring turkey seasons in Missouri. Proc. National Wild Turkey Symposium 3:176-183.

Lewis, J. B. 1978. State wild turkey survey: poult production and juvenile mortality. Missouri Department of Conservation. 12 pp.

Lewis, J. B. 1980. Fifteen years of wild turkey trapping, banding, and recovery data in Missouri. Proc. National Wild Turkey Symposium 4:24-31.

Lewis, J. B., and G. Kelly. 1973. Mortality associated with the spring hunting of gobblers. Pages 295-299 in G. C. Sanderson and H. C. Schultz, eds. Wild turkey management: current problems and programs. The Missouri Chapter of The Wildlife Society and University of Missouri Press, Columbia.

Lewis, J. B., and E. Kurzejeski. 1984. Wild turkey productivity and poult mortality in north central Missouri. Missouri Department of Conservation. Final Report. P-R Proj. W-13-R-38. 41 pp.

Lint, J. R. 1990. Assessment of mark-recapture models and indices to estimate population size of wild turkeys on Tallahala Wildlife Management Area. M.S. Thesis. Mississippi State Univ., Mississippi State. 255 pp.

Lint, J. R., B. D. Leopold, G. A. Hurst, and W. J. Hamrick. 1992. Determining effective study area size from marked and harvested wild turkey gobblers. J. Wildl. Manage. 56:556-562.

Lint, J. R., B. D. Leopold, and G. A. Hurst. 1995. Comparison of abundance indexes and population estimates for wild turkey gobblers. Wildl. Soc. Bull. 23:164-168.

Little, T. W., J. M. Kienzler, and G. A. Hanson. 1990. Effects of fall either-sex hunting on survival in an Iowa wild turkey population. Proc. National Wild Turkey Symposium 6:119-125.

Little, T. W., and K. L. Varland. 1981. Reproduction and dispersal of transplanted wild turkeys in Iowa. J. Wildl. Manage. 45:419-427.

Lobdell, C. H., K. E. Case, and H. S. Mosby. 1972. Evaluation of harvest strategies for a simulated wild turkey population. J.Wildl. Manage. 36:493-497.

Marion, W. R., T. E. O'Meara, and D. S. Maehr. 1981. Use of playback recordings in sampling elusive or secretive birds. Pages 81-85 *in* C. J. Ralph and J. M. Scott, eds. Estimating numbers of terrestrial birds. Studies in Avian Biology No. 6. Cooper Ornithological Society, Los Angeles.

McClure, H. E. 1939. Cooing activity and censusing of the mourning dove. J. Wildl. Manage. 3:323-328.

McCullough, D. R. 1979. The George Reserve deer herd. University of Michigan Press, Ann Arbor.

McDonald, L. L. 1993. Line transect sampling. *In* L. L. McDonald and B. F. J. Manly, eds. Workshop notes on statistics for field ecology.

Menzel, K. E. 1975. Population and harvest data for Merriam's turkeys in Nebraska. Proc. National Wild Turkey Symposium 3:184-188.

Miller, D. A. 1997. Habitat relationships and demographic parameters of an eastern wild turkey population in central Mississippi. Ph.D. Diss. Mississippi State University, Mississippi State. 307 pp.

Miller, D. A., L. W. Burger, B. D. Leopold, and G. A. Hurst. 1998a. Survival and cause specific mortality of wild turkey hens in central Mississippi. J. Wildl. Manage. 62:306-313.

Miller, D. A., G. A. Hurst, and B. D. Leopold. 1997. Chronology of wild turkey nesting, gobbling, and hunting in Mississippi. J. Wildl. Manage. 61:840-845.

Miller, D. A., B. D. Leopold, and G. A. Hurst. 1998b. Reproductive characteristics of a wild turkey population in central Mississippi. J. Wildl. Manage. 62:903-910.

Minta, S., and M. Mangel. 1989. A simple population estimate based on simulation for capture-recapture and capture-resight data. Ecology 70:1738-1751.

Mosby, H. S. 1967. Population dynamics. Pages 113-136 *in* O. H. Hewitt, ed. The wild turkey and its management. The Wildlife Society, Washington, D.C.

Mosby, H. S., and C. O. Handley. 1943. The wild turkey in Virginia: its status, life history, and management. Virginia Commission of Game and Inland Fisheries, Richmond.

Myers, G. T. 1973. The wild turkey on the Uncompahgre Plateau. Colorado Division of Wildlife, Denver. Final Report Fed. Aid in Wildl. Restoration Proj. W-37-R, Work Plan 2, Jobs 10 and 14. 153 pp.

Naugle, D. E., J. A. Jenks, and B. J. Kernohan. 1996. Use of thermal infrared sensing to estimate density of white-tailed deer. Wildl. Soc. Bull. 24:37-43.

Neff, D. J. 1968. The pellet-group count technique for big game trend, census, and distribution: a review. J. Wildl. Manage. 32:597-614.

Nichols, J. D., M. J. Conroy, D. R. Anderson, and K. P. Burnham. 1984. Compensatory mortality in waterfowl populations: a review of evidence and implications for research and management. Trans. North American Wildlife and Natural Resources Conf. 49:535-554.

Norman, G. W., and D. E. Steffen. 1996. 1995 Virginia spring gobbler season survey. Wildlife Resources Bull. No. 96-2:1-33.

Norton-Griffiths, M. 1978. Counting animals. African Wildlife Leadership Foundation, Nairobi, Kenya.

Novak, J. M., K. T. Scribner, W. D. Dupont, and M. H. Smith. 1991. Catch-effort estimation of white-tailed deer population size. J. Wildl. Manage. 55:31-38.

Ontario Ministry of Natural Resources. 1985. Population monitoring techniques for Ontario wild turkeys. Ontario Ministry of Natural Resources, Wildlife Branch. 23 pp.

Otis, D. L., K. P. Burnham, G. C. White, and D. R. Anderson. 1978. Statistical inference from capture data on closed animal populations. Wildl. Monogr. 62:1-35.

Overton, W. S., and D. E. Davis. 1969. Estimating the numbers of animals in wildlife populations. Pages 403-455 *in* R. H. Giles, Jr., ed. Wildlife management techniques manual. The Wildlife Society, Washington, D.C.

Pack, J. C. 1986. Report on wild turkey hunting regulations, harvest trends and population levels in West Virginia. West Virginia Division of Natural Resources, Elkins. 24 pp.

Pack, J. C. 1993. Wild turkey. Pages 1-8 *in* 1993 West Virginia Big Game Bulletin. West Virginia Division of Natural Resources, Charleston.

Pack, J. C. 1994. Analysis of the proposal to open squirrel and turkey season on the same date. West Virginia Division of Natural Resources, Charleston. 7 pp.

Pack, J. C., L. Berry, J. Evans, J. R. Hill, R. Knotts, and C. Taylor. 1995. Strategy for implementing fall hunting of wild turkeys into additional counties. West Virginia Division of Natural Resources, Elkins. 15 pp.

Paisley, R. N., R. G. Wright, and J. F. Kubisiak. 1996. Survival of wild turkey gobblers in southwestern Wisconsin. Proc. National Wild Turkey Symposium 7:39-44.

Paisley, R. N., R. G. Wright, J. F. Kubisiak, and R. E. Rolley. 1998. Reproductive ecology of eastern wild turkeys in southwestern Wisconsin. J. Wildl. Manage. 62:911-916.

Palmer, W. E., G. A. Hurst, and J. R. Lint. 1990. Effort, success, and characteristics of spring turkey hunters on Tallahala Wildlife Management Area, Mississippi. Proc. National Wild Turkey Symposium 6:208-213.

Pattee, O. H., and S. L. Beasom. 1979. Supplemental feeding to increase wild turkey productivity. J. Wildl. Manage. 43:512-516.

Paulick, G. J., and D.S. Robson. 1969. Statistical calculations for change-in-ratio estimates of population parameters. J. Wildl. Manage. 33:1-27.

Pelham, P. H., and J. G. Dickson. 1992. Physical characteristics. Pages 32-45 *in* J. G. Dickson, ed. The wild turkey: biology and management. Stackpole Books, Harrisburg, Pa.

Pollock, K. H. 1981. Capture-recapture models allowing for age-dependent survival and capture rates. Biometrics 37:521-529.

Pollock, K. H., and W. L. Kendall. 1987. Visibility bias in aerial surveys: a review of estimation procedures. J. Wildl. Manage. 51:502-520.

Pollock, K. H., R. A. Lancia, M. C. Conner, and B. L. Wood. 1985. A new change-in-ratio procedure robust to unequal catchability of types of animal. Biometrics 41:653-662.

Pollock, K. H., J. D. Nichols, C. Brownie, and J. E. Hines. 1990. Statistical inference for capture-recapture experiments. Wildl. Monogr. 107:1-97.

Porter, W. F. 1978. The ecology and behavior of the wild turkey *(Meleagris gallopavo)* in southeastern Minnesota. Ph.D. Diss. Univ. of Minnesota, St. Paul. 129 pp.

Porter, W. F., D. J. Gefell, and H. B. Underwood. 1990a. Influence of hunter harvest on the population dynamics of wild turkeys in New York. Proc. National Wild Turkey Symposium 6:188-195.

Porter, W. F., and J. R. Ludwig. 1980. Use of gobbling counts to monitor the distribution and abundance of wild turkeys. Proc. National Wild Turkey Symposium 4:61-68.

Porter, W. F., G. C. Nelson, and K. Mattson. 1983. Effects of winter conditions on reproduction in a northern wild turkey population. J. Wildl. Manage. 47:281-290.

Porter, W. F., H. B. Underwood, and D. J. Gefell. 1990b. Application of population modeling techniques to wild turkey management. Proc. National Wild Turkey Symposium 6:107-118.

Quang, P. X., and E. F. Becker. 1996. Line transect sampling under various conditions with application to aerial surveys. Ecology 77:1297-1302.

Rabinowitz, A. 1993. Wildlife field research and conservation training manual. Paul-Art Press Inc., New York.

Ridpath, M. G., R. J. Begg, M. L. Dudzinski, M. A. Forbes, and A. Graham. 1983. Counting the same populations of large tropical mammals from the ground and from the air. Australian Wildlife Research 10:487-498.

Roberts, S. D., J. M. Coffey, and W. F. Porter. 1995. Survival and reproduction of female wild turkeys in New York. J. Wildl. Manage. 59:437-447.

Roberts, S. D., and W. F. Porter. 1996. Importance of demographic parameters to annual changes in wild turkey abundance. Proc. National Wild Turkey Symposium 7:15-20.

Roberts, S. D., and W. F. Porter. 1998a. Relation between weather and survival of wild turkey nests. J.Wildl. Mange. 62:1492-1498.

Roberts, S. D., and W. F. Porter. 1998b. Influence of temperature and precipitation on survival of wild turkey poults. J. Wildl. Manage. 62:1499-1505.

Robson, D. S., and H. A. Regier. 1964. Sample size in Petersen mark-recapture experiments. Trans. Am. Fish. Soc. 93:215-226.

Rolley, R., and J. Kubisiak. 1994. Gun deer hunter turkey observation survey 1993. Wis. Wildl. Surveys 4:26-31.

Rolley, R. E., J. F. Kubisiak, R. N. Paisley, and R. G. Wright. 1998. Wild turkey population dynamics in southwestern Wisconsin. J. Wildl. Manage. 62:917-924.

Rusch, D. H., and L. B. Keith. 1971. Seasonal and annual trends in numbers of Alberta ruffed grouse. J. Wildl. Manage. 35:804-822.

Sauder, D. W., R. L. Linder, R. B. Dahlgren, and W. L. Tucker. 1971. An evaluation of the roadside technique for censusing breeding waterfowl. J. Wildl. Manage. 35:538-543.

Scattergood, L. W. 1954. Estimating fish and wildlife populations: a survey of methods. Pages 273-285 *in* O. Kempthorne, T. A. Bancroft, J. W. Gowen, and J. L. Lush, eds. Statistics and mathematics in biology. Iowa State College Press, Ames.

Schorger, A. W. 1957. The beard of the wild turkey. Auk 74:441-446.

Schorger, A. W. 1966. The wild turkey: its history and domestication. University of Oklahoma Press, Norman.

Schultz, V., and R. D. McDowell. 1957. Some comments on a wild turkey brood survey. J. Wildl. Manage. 21:85-89.

Scott, V. E., and E. L. Boeker. 1972. An evaluation of wild turkey call counts in Arizona. J. Wildl. Manage. 36:628-630.

Seber, G. A. F. 1973. The estimation of animal abundance and related parameters. Hafner Press, New York.

Seber, G. A. F. 1982. The estimation of animal abundance and related parameters. Macmillan Publishing Co., Inc., New York.

Seber, G. A. F., ed. 1985. Approximate unbiased estimation in the multisample single-recapture census. Springer-Verlag, New York.

Seber, G. A. F. 1986. A review of estimating animal abundance. Biometrics 42:267-292.

Shaw, H. G. 1973. The roadside survey for Merriam's turkeys in Arizona. Pages 285-293 *in* G. C. Sanderson and H. C. Schultz, eds. Wild turkey management: current problems and programs. The Missouri Chapter of The Wildlife Society and University of Missouri Press, Columbia.

Shaw, H. G., and R. H. Smith. 1977. Habitat use patterns of Merriam's turkey in Arizona. Ariz. Game and Fish Dep., Phoenix. Final Rep. Fed. Aid Proj. W-78-R.

Shupe, T. E., F. S. Guthery, and S. L. Beasom. 1987. Use of helicopters to survey northern bobwhite populations on rangeland. Wild. Soc. Bull. 15:458-462.

Skalski, J. R., and D. S. Robson. 1992. Techniques for wildlife investigations: design and analysis of capture data. Academic Press, Inc., San Diego, Calif.

Smith, D. M. 1975. Behavioral factors influencing variability of roost counts for Rio Grande turkeys. Proc. National Wild Turkey Symposium 3:170-175.

Smith, R. H. 1962. Statewide investigations: turkey population trend techniques. Ariz. Game and Fish Dep., Phoenix. Job Completion Rep. Fed. Aid Proj. W-78-R-7.

Speake, D. W. 1980. Predation on wild turkeys in Alabama. Proc. National Wild Turkey Symposium 4:86-101.

Speake, D. W., T. E. Lynch, W. J. Fleming, G. A. Wright, and W. J. Hamrick. 1975. Habitat use and seasonal movements of wild turkeys in the Southeast. Proc. National Wild Turkey Symposium 3:122-130.

Stauffer, D. F. 1993. Quail methodology: where are we and where do we need to be? Pages 21-33 *in* K. E. Church and T. V. Dailey, eds. Quail III: National Quail Symposium. Kansas Dep. Wildl. and Parks, Pratt.

Steffen, D. E., and G. W. Norman. 1996. Dynamics between spring and fall harvests of wild turkeys in Virginia. Proc. National Wild Turkey Symposium 7:231-237.

Stirling, I., and J. F. Bendell. 1966. Census of blue grouse with recorded calls of a female. J. Wildl. Manage. 30:184-187.

Stokes, A. W., and D. F. Balph. 1965. The relation of animal behavior to wildlife management. Trans. North Am. Wildl. Nat. Resour. Conf. 30:401-410.

Stott, R. S., and D. P. Olson. 1972. An evaluation of waterfowl surveys on the New Hampshire coastline. J. Wildl. Manage. 36:468-477.

Suchy, W. J., W. R. Clark, and T. W. Little. 1983. Influence of simulated harvest on Iowa wild turkey populations. Proc. Iowa Acad. Sci. 90:98-102.

Suchy, W. J., G. A. Hanson, and T. W. Little. 1990. Evaluation of a population model as a management tool in Iowa. Proc. National Wild Turkey Symposium 6:196-204.

Taylor, C. I., G. H. Sharp, J. E. Evans, J. C. Pack, and W. K. Igo. 1998. 1997 spring gobbler survey. West Virginia Division of Natural Resources, Wildlife Resources Section, Elkins. 27 pp.

Tefft, B. C. 1996a. 1995 wild turkey status report. Rhode Island Dep. Environmental Management, West Kingston. 11 pp.

Tefft, B. C. 1996b. Rhode Island wild turkey study. Rhode Island Dep. Environmental Management, West Kingston. 7 pp.

Vander-Haegen, W. M. 1987. Population dynamics and habitat preferences of wild turkeys in western Massachusetts. M. S. Thesis. University of Massachusetts, Amherst. 67 pp.

Vangilder, L. D. 1992. Population dynamics. Pages 144-164 *in* J. G. Dickson, ed. The wild turkey: biology and management. Stackpole Books, Harrisburg, Pa.

Vangilder, L. D. 1996. Survival and cause-specific mortality of wild turkeys in the Missouri Ozarks. Proc. National Wild Turkey Symposium 7:21-31.

Vangilder, L. D., and T. G. Kulowiec. 1988. Documentation for Missouri Department of Conservation turkey population model. Missouri Department of Conservation, Columbia. 19 pp.

Vangilder, L. D., and E. W. Kurzejeski. 1995. Population ecology of the eastern wild turkey in northern Missouri. Wildl. Monogr. 130:1-50.

Verner, J., ed. 1985. Assessment of counting techniques. Plenum Press, New York.

Watts, C. R., and A. W. Stokes. 1971. The social order of turkeys. Scientific American 224:112-118.

Weaver, J., and K. Bellamy. 1989. Winter wild turkey census, Napanee District, Ontario, February/March 1989. Ontario Ministry of Natural Resources.

Weaver, J. K., and H. S. Mosby. 1979. Influence of hunting regulations on Virginia wild turkey populations. J. Wildl. Manage. 43:128-135.

Weinrich, J., E. E. Langenau, Jr., and T. Reis. 1985. Relationship between winter census and spring harvest of wild turkeys in northern lower Michigan. Proc. National Wild Turkey Symposium 5:295-301.

Weinstein, M., B. D. Leopold, and G. A. Hurst. 1995. Evaluation of wild turkey population estimation methods. Proc. Annu. Conf. Southeast. Assoc. Fish and Wildl. Agencies 49:476-487.

Weinstein, M., D. A. Miller, L. M. Connor, B. D. Leopold, and G. A. Hurst. 1996. What affects turkeys? A conceptual model for future research. Proc. National Wild Turkey Symposium 7:135-142.

Welsh, R. J., and R. O. Kimmel. 1990. Turkey sightings by hunters of antlerless deer as an index to wild turkey abundance in Minnesota. Proc. National Wild Turkey Symposium 6:126-133.

White, G. C. 1996. NOREMARK: population estimation from mark-resighting surveys. Wildl. Soc. Bull. 24:50-52.

White, G. C., D. R. Anderson, K. P. Burnham, and D. L. Otis. 1982. Capture-recapture and removal methods for sampling closed populations. Los Alamos National Laboratory, Los Alamos, N.M. 235pp.

White, G. C., K. P. Burnham, D. L. Otis, and D. R. Anderson. 1978. User's manual for program CAPTURE. Utah State University Press, Logan. 40 pp.

Williams, L. E., Jr., and D. H. Austin. 1988. Studies of the wild turkey in Florida. Fla. Game and Fresh Water Fish Comm. Div. Wildl. Tech. Bull. 10:1-210.

Williams, L. E., Jr., D. H. Austin, and T. E. Peoples. 1980. Turkey nesting success on a Florida study area. Proc. National Wild Turkey Symposium 4:102-107.

Wise, G. D. 1973. Restoration of the wild turkey in Indiana. Pages 65-69 in G. C. Sanderson and H. C. Schultz, eds. Wild turkey management: current problems and programs. Missouri Chapter of The Wildlife Society and University of Missouri Press, Columbia.

Wooley, J. B., D. D. Humberg, A. L. Farris, R. R. George, and J. M. Kienzler. 1978. Analysis of ring-necked pheasant population surveys. Iowa Wildl. Res. Bull. No. 24:1-22.

Wunz, G. A. 1986. Where do we go from here? Turkey Call 13:26-29.

Wunz, G. A., and A. H. Hayden. 1975. Winter mortality and supplemental feeding of turkeys in Pennsylvania. Proc. National Wild Turkey Symposium 3:61-69.

Wunz, G. A., and A. S. Ross. 1990. Wild turkey production, fall and spring harvest interactions, and responses to harvest management in Pennsylvania. Proc. National Wild Turkey Symposium 6:205-207.

Wunz, G. A., and W. K. Shope. 1980. Turkey brood survey in Pennsylvania as it relates to harvest. Proc. National Wild Turkey Symposium 4:69-75.

Zirkle, J. W. 1982. Wild turkeys. Pages 73-74 in D. E. Davis, ed. CRC handbook of census methods for terrestrial vertebrates. CRC Press, Inc., Boca Raton, Fla.

Appendix A.

Minnesota spring wild turkey population and hunting permit allocation model.
R. O. Kimmel, 1998. Minnesota Department of Natural Resources, Rt. 1, Box 181, Madelia, MN 56062, phone 507-642-8478, e-mail richard.kimmel@dnr.state.mn.us

Minnesota Department of Natural Resources regulates spring wild turkey hunting by area and time period. For the spring 1999 turkey season, hunters applied to hunt during 1 of 8, 5-day time periods (between April 14 and May 23) and in 1 of 36 Permit Areas. More than 35,000 applications were received for 18,360 available permits.

When turkey hunting was initiated in Minnesota in 1978, the number of available hunting permits was held at low levels to maintain a minimal harvest because of a developing wild turkey population. As Minnesota's turkey population and hunter interest increased, the number of available permits was increased requiring a systematic approach to setting permit levels. The mathematical model I describe incorporates available information to estimate the turkey population for the previous spring and for the upcoming spring hunting seasons, and to calculate the optimal number of hunting permits to issue to meet management objectives.

Program Goal — to issue the maximum number of turkey hunting permits without harming the resource or reducing the quality of hunting.

Factors considered in model:

1) **Turkey Population Factors**
- previous harvest — to estimate the previous spring population
- population indices — to estimate the change in population over time; the population trend

2) **Quality Factors**
- habitat distribution
- hunter interference rates

Other factors (such as size of permit areas, number of hunters and harvest success rates from past hunts, and problems of hunter access to private land) are also considered before making final determinations.

Turkey Population Factors

1. Estimate the previous spring turkey population for each permit area (PSP = previous spring population).

PSP = Registered Harvest / fraction of population harvested

We assume that the registered harvest represents 15% of the spring population. Past models used 10%, as indicated from past wild turkey research (e.g., Lewis and Kelly 1973). However, more recent information for Wisconsin, with a season framework similar to Minnesota's spring season, indicates 16% of the population was harvested (Paisley et al. 1996). We plan to refine this value for Minnesota.

2. Determine population trend

We use percent of "hunters observing wild turkeys" (HOWT), from a survey of turkey observations by deer hunters, as a population index (Welsh and Kimmel 1990, Kimmel et al. 1996b). Population indices from the 3 most recent population surveys are used to determine the population trend or HOWT change.

3. Estimate the turkey population for each permit area for the upcoming spring turkey hunting season (FSP = future spring population).

FSP = PSP x HOWT change

4. Estimate the gobbler population using future spring population and % males in the population. We assume % males is 46% from Minnesota pheasant modeling (another males-only hunted species) (A. Berner, pers. commun.).

gobblers = FSP x 0.46

5. Set goal — Minnesota's current harvest goal (acceptable harvest) is 30% of males for all permit areas.

6. Calculate the number of permits to issue for each permit area to achieve the harvest goal using the estimated gobbler population, previous year's hunter success and the assumed % of permit recipients (95%) that actually hunt as determined by turkey hunter surveys (Kimmel et al. 1996a). This projects recommended number of permits to issue based on the estimated turkey population. (Quality factors are taken into consideration in steps 7-9.)

Quality Factor

7. Habitat Distribution (HD) factors are developed from Geographic Information System (GIS) maps of forest cover. Amount and spatial distribution of forest cover are subjectively evaluated for each permit area. This factor becomes a multiplier; i.e. factors <1 reduce the permit numbers.

Habitat Distribution	Factor
Good (Permit Area 349)	1.0
Moderate-plus	0.8
Moderate (Permit Area 225)	0.7
Moderate-minus	0.6
Limited (Permit Area 450)	0.5

8. Interference Rate (IR) factors are determined from turkey hunter survey data (Kimmel et al. 1996a). Factors are based on interference rates and used as multipliers as with Habitat Distribution.

Interference Rate	Factor
>25%	0.7
>20% - 25%	0.8
>15% - 20%	1.0
</ = 15%	1.2

9. The number of hunting permits recommended for each permit area is determined using permit numbers based on population estimate, Habitat Distribution, and Interference Rates.

Recommended Permits = Permits (step 6) x HD x IR

The recommended number of permits for each area is compared to the number of permits offered in past years. The wildlife manager, however, makes the final decision for permit numbers to be offered for permit areas within his or her work area.

Spreadsheet Columns

Column A — Permit Area Number

Column B — Registered Harvest for Spring 1998 Turkey Season

Column C — Previous Spring Population (PSP) (Column B/0.15)

Column D — Population index (HOWT) for 3rd most recent survey

Column E — Population index for 2nd most recent survey

Column F — Population index for most recent survey

Column G — Annual population trend (HOWT change) calculated from D, E, F; formula takes into consideration the number of years between each pair of surveys

Column H — Estimate of future spring population (FSP) (C x G)

Column I — Forest abundance - mi² of forest cover in the permit area (% forest cover (GIS data) x total mi² in permit area)

Column J — Gobblers per mi² in the permit area ((H x 0.46) / I)

Column K — Harvest goal expressed as % of males

Column L — Number of permits **issued** during previous hunt

Column M — Hunter success during previous hunt (B/L)

Column N — Number hunters per mi² of forest to achieve harvest goal ((K x J) / M)

Column O — Number of permits to issue for each Permit Area to achieve goal ((N x I) / 0.95) - assumes 95% of permit recipients actually hunt

Note — Square miles of habitat is actually entered into the model for comparison between permit areas. This value enters the model in column J and is then removed from the model in Column O.

Column P — Hunters per season (for 8 season framework) to achieve population goal (Column O / 8)

Column Q — Permits issued per season for previous year's turkey hunting season. This is listed for comparison to columns P and R.

Note — Column R is **model value** for number of permits to issue

Column R — Number of turkey hunting permits to issue per season which includes both population and quality factors (P x S x T)

Column S — Habitat Distribution factor (HD)

Column T— Interference Rate factor (IR)

Column U — Number of permits actually issued following input from local wildlife managers and the public. This would ideally fall between the model value (column R) and the number of permits issued for the previous year's hunting season (column Q).

Column V — Hunter density - hunters per square mile of forest placed in each permit area (U / I).

Literature Cited

Kimmel, R.O., G.C. Nelson, and S.L. McDonald. 1996a. Spring 1996 wild turkey hunter survey. Pages 54-58 *in* B. Joselyn, ed. Summaries of wildlife research findings 1996. Minnesota Department of Natural Resources, Section of Wildlife. St. Paul.

Kimmel, R.O., J.H. Poate, and M.R. Riggs. 1996b. Spatial handling of wild turkey survey data using Geographic Information System mapping procedures. Proc. National Wild Turkey Symposium 7:219-223.

Lewis, J.B., and G. Kelly. 1973. Mortality associated with the spring hunting of gobblers. Pages 295-299 *in* G.C. Sanderson and H.C. Schultz, eds., Wild turkey Management: current problems and programs. University of Missouri Press, Columbia.

Paisley, R.N., R.G. Wright, and J.F. Kubisiak. 1996. Survival of wild turkey gobblers in southwestern Wisconsin. Proc. National Wild Turkey Symposium 7:39-44.

Welsh, R.J., and R.O. Kimmel. 1990. Turkey sightings by hunters of antlerless deer as an index to wild turkey abundance in Minnesota. Proc. National wild Turkey Symposium 6:126-133.

Appendix B.

Strategy for implementing fall hunting of wild turkeys into additional counties.
Adapted from J.C. Pack, L. Berry, J. Evans, J.R. Hill, R. Knotts, and C. Taylor. 1995. West Virginia Division of
Natural Resources, Wildlife Resources Section.

Wild Turkey Regulation Strategy

All counties currently closed to fall turkey hunting will
remain closed until the county has a spring harvest of
**1 bird per square mile of turkey range for a
minimum of 2 years in succession.** The county must
also be adjacent to a county which now has fall turkey
hunting or it must be **adjacent to 2 other counties**
which have a spring harvest of at least 1 bird per
square mile for 2 years in succession.

Any county qualifying for fall hunting will initially be
opened to 6 days of either-sex hunting with a limited
number of permits. The season will open the same
date as the traditional fall hunted counties. Any
county opened must maintain a spring gobbler kill of
at least 1 bird per square mile of range to remain
open.

Only resident hunters will be permitted to participate
in hunting in counties open to permit hunting. All
resident hunters except landowners will be required to
apply for permits.

Other calculations used in issuing permits are as
follows:

1. Permit numbers will be based on maintaining a
maximum fall harvest of no more than 5 percent of the
turkey population.

2. Population levels are based on spring gobbler
harvests which are equal to 10 percent of the total
population.

3. Hunting success is 27 percent.
4. Permit allocations and counties to be open for a
current year will be adjusted by brood reports and
mast data available by September prior to opening of
a fall season.

5. Permit numbers will be adjusted based on the
anticipated number of landowners.

Proposed Time Schedule

Operation of Turkey Permit System
1. Proposed counties to have permit system to be
presented at Sportsmen Meetings in March.

2. Proposed counties to be presented to Natural
Resources Commissioners in April for approval with
the understanding that modifications may be
necessary based on May Gobbler Harvest.

3. In June, Spring Gobbler Harvest Data are used to
correct the county list. Counties are added or
subtracted depending on whether or not they meet the
harvest goal of 1 gobbler per square mile for 2
successive years. To be added to the list a county must
also be adjacent to a fall hunt county or 2 adjacent
counties that also qualify for the first time.

4. Permit availability to be announced by July 1 with
information on applications, deadline for receiving
applications, planned number of permits available, etc.

5. Commissioners will be informed of progress of
system and specifics on numbers available at July
meeting.

6. The number of permits to be issued will seldom
change after July, but the system must include the
option to revise permit allocations based on brood
reports and mast condition information available in
September. This part of the system is vital to open
additional counties for fall hunting.

7. Permits will be mailed no later than October 1.

Appendix C.

Advantages, disadvantages, cost and manpower notes on wild turkey population censusing, estimating, and indexing methods. Notes particularly applicable or worth special consideration for wild turkeys in the Northeast are in italics.

I. Census Techniques

Method	Advantages	Disadvantages	Cost	Manpower
Direct winter counts (e.g. interviewing cooperators) (includes **roost counts**) This method may be better classified as an index (see Caughley 1977a:24-25), except in certain populations where all turkeys associate into flocks.	• Estimates of population size were correlated with the following spring's harvest in MI (Weinrich et al. 1985). • Supplemental foods in winter attract birds, thus resulting in greater visibility. • *Provides a total count rather than an index, which makes it easier to explain to the public, media, and legislature (Weinrich et al. 1985).* • Involves an entire area rather than a sampling for statistical expansion to area estimates (Weinrich et al. 1985). • Not very labor intensive • Use of cooperating landowners limits access problems that might arise from other censusing methods (Weinrich et al. 1985). • Where roosting patterns are stable, may be a reliable inventory method (Cook 1973). • "Turkey flocks, being relatively conspicuous, attract attention and create interest among local residents so that observations of flocks made by reliable persons can be valuable..." (Hoffman 1962). • An advantage of counting the number of animals per group is that mean group size can be calculated very accurately and with high repeatability (Caughley 1977a:25). • Use of cooperators can provide data from a relatively large area (e.g., an entire state). • *Works well in areas with severe winters where weather conditions restrict movement of the birds (Weinrich et al. 1985, as cited in Ontario 1985).* • Short census period limits movements between flocks and is not labor intensive (Ontario 1985).	• In TX, flocks moved to different winter roosts, resulting in double sampling by landowners (Cook 1973); this can be minimized by a short census period (Weinrich et al. 1985). • Except under rare circumstances such as winter flocking in northern MI and traditional roost sites in TX, direct counts have limited feasibility (Kurzejeski and Vangilder 1992). • Landowner interest may decline over the years, with individuals responding less frequently (Welsh and Kimmel 1990). • The correlation between winter census and spring kill is affected by sex and age composition, dispersal patterns, land ownership and use, and weather (Weinrich et al. 1985). • In TX, instability of roost sites and infrequent observations caused many landowners to make inaccurate estimates of turkey numbers (Cook 1973). • In TX, roosting patterns were so variable and unstable that roost counts were not reliable estimators of the winter population (Smith 1975). • Midwinter movements were problematic in MN (Porter 1978) • Unstable roosting patterns can be produced by (1) human activity and land use practices, (2) relative availability of roost sites, (3) heightened sensitivity of small flocks. • Winter concentration counts were not correlated with other survey methods in NE (Menzel 1975). • The regression of density on group size is seldom linear and it usually cuts the vertical axis below the origin; hence the index ranks densities but does not reveal the proportional difference between them (Caughley 1977a:25).		• 6-8 people full time for a 2-week period to collect data from cooperators, in MI (Weinrich et al. 1985).

Method	Advantages	Disadvantages	Cost	Manpower
Aerial counts (Beasom 1970, in TX) NOTE: Some investigators treat aerial surveys as relative (i.e., indices) rather than absolute measures of abundance (Caughley and Goddard 1972 as cited in Ontario 1985, Eberhardt 1978b). May be considered a subset of plot/quadrat sampling or transect sampling (Krebs 1989).	• Useful in open habitats. • Permits direct counts of individuals. • Causes less disturbance than ground surveys (Caughley 1977a:38). • A practical method over large areas (Ontario 1985). "The only practicable means of estimating the number of large animals inhabiting an extensive area on land or in the sea" (Seber 1982:454, Caughley 1977b). • *Useful (considering cost and logistics) for extensive inaccessible areas and on a broad scale (Ridpath et al. 1983).* • Requires little manpower and time (Caughley 1974b as cited in Ontario 1985). • *Could be conducted in winter to determine the distribution of a new population (Ontario 1985).* • May be used in conjunction with ground surveys to improve the accuracy of population estimates (Caughley 1974b as cited in Ontario 1985) [see **Double sampling**]. • Ground counts are only practicable when there is good access and visibility and when the animals are reasonably tame to vehicles (Norton-Griffiths 1978:94) [aerial surveys largely circumvent these problems]. • "Although the estimate is usually inaccurate and often imprecise it answers a broad range of ecological and management questions to an acceptable level of approximation" (Caughley 1977b).	• *Limited utility in heavily vegetated areas* • Ability to see the animals may vary among individual observers (Scattergood 1954). • Animals may stay tend to stay under cover with certain weather conditions or at certain times of the day). • Speed of airplane, height above ground, transect width, and skill of different observers have significant effects on population estimates (Seber 1982, Caughley et al. 1976, Caughley 1977b, Norton-Griffiths 1978, Eberhardt et al. 1979, Ridpath et al. 1983—speed only); observed densities may not be directly comparable between different surveys (estimates) (Caughley et al. 1976). • Variation of pilots (Hoskinson 1976), snow conditions, terrain, and time of day appear to bias results (LeResche and Rausch 1974, Davis and Winstead 1980). • Amount of cloud cover or size of aircraft affected results for coastal waterfowl (Stott and Olson 1972). • Extremely variable results in comparison with surface counts, for coastal waterfowl (Stott and Olson 1972). • *Underestimates seem to be inherent in the method (Stott and Olson 1972, LeResche and Rausch 1974) (cited in Davis and Winstead 1980) (Scattergood 1954) (Caughley 1974b, with references). This can be a problem when accurate population estimates are needed to establish harvest rates and quotas (LaResche and Rausch 1974 as cited in Ontario 1985). "Even inexperienced observers can overlook as many as 20% or more of the animals*	• \$25 per km² for aerial transects of deer in South Dakota (Naugle et al. 1996). • Shupe et al. (1987) counted bobwhite from a helicopter along transects. The cost of aerial transects was less than for mark-recapture estimates, but above the cost of conducting drive counts (cited in Stauffer 1993). • Helicopter > fixed-wing > ground (Ridpath et al. 1983, for large tropical mammals in Australia).	• Helicopter > ground > fixed-wing... When counting in wooded habitats only, the effort in counting from the ground or in a fixed-wing aircraft is much the same (Ridpath et al. 1983, for large tropical mammals in Australia).

II. Estimates (continued)

Method	Advantages	Disadvantages	Cost	Manpower
Aerial counts (continued)		*[see references in Seber 1982:456], so that all estimates, whether based on quadrats or transects are underestimates" (Seber 1982:456).* • "Animals missed in heavy cover, observer fatigue from boredom from flying over low density areas, variable snow cover and terrain, different observers in subsequent surveys, the surveyors' competency or level of experience, and pilot interest, attitude, and skill all result in low population estimates" (Ontario 1985). • Provide only a rough estimate of population size (Ontario 1985). • Aerial summer census with helicopters was not recommended by Myers (1973) in CO. • Fixed-wing plane census in winter at feed stations was unsuccessful in CO (Myers 1973) • Usually cannot be used to estimate densities of birds, because birds are easily missed and because one normally cannot relate flocks sampled to total area sampled (Verner 1985). • The resulting estimate "is usually inaccurate, biased, and often imprecise (i.e. has large variance)" [but] can be used to answer a broad range of ecological and management questions to an acceptable level of approximation (Seber 1982). • Ground counts are more useful for obtaining data on the seasonal patterns of distribution within different vegetation types, and also provides information on the behavior and condition of the animals that cannot be obtained from aircraft (Norton-Griffiths 1978). • "Counting from the ground is the only method suitable to obtain detailed demographic and environmental data of the population. It may be a cheap alternative to the use of aircraft where the area is small enough (as Norton-Griffiths 1978) and access is feasible (Ridpath et al. 1983). • Ground vehicles travel more slowly and counting rate is higher (Norton-Griffiths 1978:94). • Ground vehicles can stop as necessary to make highly accurate counts, and can make incidental observations on behavior, age and sex structure, condition, state of the vegetation, etc. (Norton-Griffiths 1978:94).		

Method	Advantages	Disadvantages	Cost	Manpower
Line transects	• Compensates for differences in observability along survey routes, compared with strip transects (DeYoung and Priebe 1987). • All animals observed in a survey are used in forming an estimate of abundance, as contrasted with strip transects (Eberhardt et al. 1979, Burnham et al. 1985, Caughley and Sinclair 1994). This tends to increase the precision of the estimate (Caughley and Sinclair 1994). • "In habitats where it is difficult to spot every animal you are looking for or for you to know that you are not scaring animals away, line transects are more appropriate than fixed-width [strip] transects" (Rabinowitz 1993) • It is not necessary to detect all animals present in the study plot. Only a small percentage of the animals actually present might be detected (Buckland et al. 1993). • Allows a relaxation of the strong assumptions required for strip (i.e., plot or quadrat) sampling (Burnham and Anderson 1984, as cited in Buckland et al. 1993). • Less expensive than mark-recapture (Buckland et al. 1993 with references). • Possible advantage for wild turkeys: this method "is perhaps more appropriate [than strip transects] when the counts are likely to be low" (Seber 1982:461). • A particularly useful method when the animals are too mobile to be sampled using sample plots, or when the animals are difficult to locate and must be flushed into the open (Seber 1982:562, Brower 1990:119). • "The line transect method will give more value for the money than quadrat sampling, provided the underlying assumptions are satisfied (Seber 1982:563). • Best suited to large areas that are relatively uniform within sections of hundreds of meters or more...Particularly suitable in extensive, open, uniform, or species-poor habitats" (Bibby et al. 1992:66,84). • Probably more accurate than point counts (Bibby et al. 1992:67). • "The major advantage of the line transect sampling scheme is the relative ease of its implementation in the field once a proper design has been chosen" Anderson et al. 1979). • "[The inclusion of objects outside a narrow strip, where	• Larger standard errors than strip transects (DeYoung and Priebe 1987). • Line transects "are known for their ease of performance in some situations, not for their accuracy and precision. Estimates of variance and computation of confidence intervals are difficult, as specific theoretical models or mathematical distributions typically must be assumed; but confidence intervals as an expression of precision of the population estimate may be expressed readily if replicate transects are sampled" (Brower 1990:120). • *Difficult to observe sufficient numbers of turkeys to derive accurate estimates.* • All animals located directly on the line must be detected (Lancia et al. 1994:231, Pollock et al. 1990:66). This may be especially difficult in aerial surveys (Pollock et al. 1990:66). • *Animals cannot move before they are sighted, and no animals can be counted twice (Lancia et al. 1994:231).* • Distances (e.g. perpendicular distance of the animal from the line) must be measured exactly (Lancia et al. 1994:231). This may be impractical, especially in aerial surveys (Pollock et al. 1990:66). "Studies based on sighting distances and angles are generally subject to more severe biases" (McDonald 1993). • Sightings must be independent events (e.g., the flushing of one animal does not cause another to flush) (Lancia et al. 1994:231). • Animals must be detected or missed in random fashion (Quang and Becker 1996). • Probability of detection must depend only on distance (Quang and Becker 1996).	• Shupe et al. (1987) counted bobwhite from a helicopter along transects. The cost of aerial transects was less than for mark-recapture estimates, but above the cost of conducting drive counts (cited in Stauffer 1993). • Mark recapture exceeded costs for walking line transects by a factor of three in rangeland studies in TX (Shupe et al. 1987, as cited in Buckland et al. 1993). • Labor is comparable to estimates based on the Lincoln-Petersen index (Guthery 1988). • For a study on northern bobwhites in Texas, cost was about $47/km to establish transects, plus $3.30 to sample them (Guthery 1988).	• For a study on northern bobwhites in Texas, labor involved about 4.7 hours per km to establish transects on moderately brushy rangeland (using a crew of 3 using a chainsaw, bow saw, and limb cutters), plus 17-23 minutes per km for sampling (Guthery 1988).

Method	Advantages	Disadvantages	Cost	Manpower
Line transects (continued)	detection is less than perfect] and the ability to collect and analyze grouped data (rather than individual distance) represent major advantages of line transect over strip transect sampling" (Burnham and Anderson 1984). "Line transect width may be large (effectively unbounded) and the number counted (sample size, n) typically much greater than on a narrow strip transect" (Burnham et al. 1985). • Advantage over strip transects: "Strip data often result in biased estimates because objects in the strip are missed" (Burnham and Anderson 1984). • *Advantage over strip transects: "A properly conducted line transect survey will provide valid estimates of density even if a substantial fraction of objects go undetected" (Burnham and Anderson 1984).* • Advantage over strip transects: "The results [of this paper's analysis] indicate a preference for the line transect survey method over strip transects on the basis of bias and efficiency...The results show that line transect sampling generally has a smaller MSE than strip transect sampling...Bias does not increase as transect width increases" (Burnham et al. 1985). • Line transect "indices are efficient in that they collect a large amount of data quickly and with relatively small effort" (Brower 1990).	• Detection of animals may depend on distance, group size, environmental conditions, time of day, and animal behavior (Buckland et al. 1993, Quang and Becker 1996). • Likely to be more appropriate in relatively heterogeneous habitats such as rangelands, as opposed to patchy habitats such as croplands (Stauffer 1993, in a paper on quail). • Requires a greater investment of time and effort than methods to derive indices (Stauffer 1993, in a paper about quail). • *Transects are not practical for species that occur at such low densities that you are not able to obtain a reasonable sample size (Rabinowitz 1993); sample size of at least 25-30, and preferably 40-80, is recommended (Burnham et al. 1980).* • It is believed that the line transect sampling method can be applied only if the geometric center of the cluster can be determined adequately. Animals in **loose** groups cannot be analyzed appropriately as a clustered population because they usually do not flush simultaneously and the geometric center is nearly impossible to establish accurately (Burnham et al. 1980, Anderson et al. 1979). • For clustered populations, it may be difficult to meet the requirement that cluster size be determined accurately (Buckland et al. 1993). • Not a very good approach in small areas or for detecting the effects of fine-grained habitat variation (Bibby et al. 1992:66). • "Transect methods do not always work because dense shrub and rough terrain make it difficult for the observer to walk quietly and simultaneously look for birds" (Seber 1986). • *Large sampling effort (total distance walked) may be required for acceptable levels of precision with species such as northern bobwhites (Guthery 1988).* • "Application of transects is difficult on large areas because of time requirements" (Guthery 1988). • Accuracy "depends heavily on which model is chosen for the analysis" (Caughley and Sinclair 1994).		

Method	Advantages	Disadvantages	Cost	Manpower
Strip transects	• Simpler to use than variable-distance line transects, because one records only the birds detected within the strip...The observer must be trained to estimate only one distance accurately—that to the limit of the strip (Verner 1985). • *Strip transects "have the immense advantages of simplicity and realism. If the transect width is appropriately chosen, what the observer sees is what the observer gets. The mathematics of such sampling are simple, elegant, and absolutely solid" (Caughley and Sinclair 1994).* • Provides a density estimate (Verner 1985). • Better than line transect if animals are quite numerous (Eberhardt et al. 1979). • Statistically more accurate (unbiased) than line transects (because you are counting total numbers instead of estimating) (Rabinowitz 1993, Burnham et al. 1985). • Generally easier to locate and sample than quadrats (Seber 1986).	• Too variable over time, compared with line transects (DeYoung and Priebe 1987). • Does not meet the assumption that all individuals in the fixed-width strip were sighted. It is generally recognized that belt (strip) surveys often fail to detect 100% of the animals present in the strip when used for estimation of density (McDonald 1993). • *Difficult to observe sufficient numbers of turkeys to derive accurate estimates.* • Sample size could be small, leading to an estimator with a large variance (Burnham et al. 1985). • Animals observed outside the transect must be ignored; this could be a problem when densities are very low (Eberhardt et al. 1979) • *Not appropriate for most forest situations (Rabinowitz 1993)* • Transects are not practical for species that occur at such low densities that you are not able to obtain a reasonable sample size (Rabinowitz 1993) • *If the objects counted are either rare or not readily seen (or both), restricting coverage to a strip of definite width may require an unreasonably large number of transects to provide suitably narrow confidence-limits on an estimate (Eberhardt 1978b).* • All animals within the strip must be detected, in contrast to line transects (Buckland et al. 1993). • Possible disadvantage for wild turkeys: this method "is appropriate when the population is fairly numerous and readily visible" (Seber 1982:460). • Are more affected by boundary effects (e.g. movement of animals on the boundary) than quadrats (Seber 1986). • "Strip transects are generally inappropriate for birds because of lack of visibility" (Burnham et al. 1980, as cited in Seber 1986). • "Transect methods do not always work because dense shrub and rough terrain make it difficult for the observer to walk quietly and simultaneously look for birds" (Seber 1986). • "[The inclusion of objects outside a narrow strip, where detection is less than perfect] and the ability to collect and analyze grouped data (rather than individual distance) represent major advantages of line transect over strip transect sampling" (Burnham and Anderson 1984). • "Strip data often result in biased estimates because objects in the strip are missed" (Burnham and Anderson 1984).		

Method	Advantages	Disadvantages	Cost	Manpower
Drive counts	• Can be useful to completely count all birds on relatively small (i.e., <500 ha) areas (Stauffer 1993, in a paper on quail). • Dogs can be used to assist.	• Should not be used with animals that remain quiet or hide, or escape into trees (Rabinowitz 1993:110). • Large number of people required (Rabinowitz 1993:110).	• Shupe et al. (1987) counted bobwhite from a helicopter along transects. The cost of aerial transects was less than for mark-recapture estimates, but above the cost of conducting drive counts (cited in Stauffer 1993).	

Method	Advantages	Disadvantages	Cost	Manpower
Mark-recapture	• *Useful for estimating population size in detailed research studies (Kurzejeski and Vangilder 1992) or for evaluating indices.* • May be of some use in setting management objectives (Gribben 1986). • *"Of all the [abundance] methods considered in this book, the Petersen method appears to be most useful, provided that the assumptions underlying the method are satisfied and there are sufficient recaptures in the second sample" (Seber 1982:564).* • Can be used to provide information on birth, death, and movement rates in addition to information on absolute abundance (Krebs 1989:15, Caughley and Sinclair 1994:208). In addition to estimating population size, can be used "to investigate habitat selection and other distributions, to calculate survival rates, measure dispersal and other movements, and to measure reproductive success of individual birds" (Bibby et al. 1992:105). • In general, populations that can be sampled by either mark-recapture or removal methods are sampled more reliably and efficiently using mark-recapture procedures (Brower 1990).	• *Costly, effort-intensive, and time-consuming (Gribben 1986, Caughley 1977a:134).* • *Several assumption need to be met (e.g., the critical assumption of equal probability of recapture for marked and unmarked turkeys) (DeYoung and Priebe 1987, Kurzejeski and Vangilder 1992, Krebs 1989).* • *It is not always easy to detect departures from the assumption that marked and unmarked animals have the same probability of being caught in the second sample, which may lead to biased estimates (Seber 1982:565).* • Capture of turkeys is too difficult to result in the necessary sample sizes needed for detailed population studies (Gribben 1986). • Not an appropriate method for estimating population structure (Gribben 1986). • Different types of tags may have different recovery/retention rates (Myers 1973) [so data may be biased or non-comparable] • Very time consuming compared with other methods (Verner 1985). "Require considerable time and effort to get the required data" (Krebs 1989:16). • "Results are often inaccurate because mark-recapture models are seldom more than a vague approximation to reality" (Caughley 1977a:134). • Not very robust, and "even small deviations from their implicit assumptions can produce large errors in the results" (Caughley 1977a:134). "To be accurate, they require a set of very restrictive assumptions about the properties of the population being studied" (Krebs 1989:16). • "When animals are readily observable, observation-based methods for estimating population size often will be preferable to capture-recapture methods." • Relatively expensive, compared to line transects (Buckland et al. 1993 with references). • *Variable catchability is a common problem. Catchability can vary with age and sex, size, type of trap and its location, type of bait, and environmental conditions. The process of*	• Shupe et al. (1987) counted bobwhite from a helicopter along transects. The cost of aerial transects was less than for mark-recapture estimates, but above the cost of conducting drive counts (cited in Stauffer 1993). • Mark recapture exceeded costs for walking line transects by a factor of 3 in rangeland studies in TX (Shupe et al. 1987, as cited in Buckland et al. 1993). • Labor for Lincoln-Petersen index is comparable to estimates based on the line transect method (Guthery 1988).	

Method	Advantages	Disadvantages	Cost	Manpower
Mark-recapture (continued)		*catching and tagging, and even the tag itself, can seriously affect the subsequent catching of an animal (Seber 1982:487 with references). Unequal vulnerability of age and sex groups to harvest is a problem; estimates usually need to be made for each sex-age group—so sample sizes increase.* • *Dependence on hunters for tag return may lead to non-reporting or mis-reporting of tags, leading to an overestimate of population size (Seber 1982:489).* • A considerable proportion of the population must be marked for a reasonable accuracy... a number of authors have commented on the need to mark at least 50% of the population (Seber 1982:565 with references). • "Mark-recapture techniques are difficult to use in the real world, and you should be certain they are needed before starting to use these techniques" (Krebs 1989:59). • Since mark-recapture methods typically only serve to estimate abundance at a single plot, the statistical inference is limited to abundance of the animals in that study area, rather than for the overall contiguous population or the mean abundance of the overall area (Skalski and Robson 1992).		

Method	Advantages	Disadvantages	Cost	Manpower
Removal methods (Includes next 2 techniques: change-in-ratio and catch-effort)	• May yield more information for the same amount of effort than mark-recapture when hunters carry out the removal (Hanson 1967) [but the reverse may be true if hunters are not used (Chapman 1955)]. • When used with an index method (such as roadside surveys), the index can be used to estimate absolute density (Eberhardt 1982 as cited in Krebs 1989:162).	• Survey-removal methods (one of several types of removal methods) cannot be used when no obvious sex or age or other distinction between the classes can be readily recognized in the field (Hanson 1967). • The principal difficulty with the survey-removal method is that sex or age or other class of the population often exhibit different behavior, leading to unrepresentative samples from the field (Hanson 1967). • In general, populations that can be sampled by either mark-recapture or removal methods are sampled more reliably and efficiently using mark-recapture procedures (Brower 1990).		
Change-in-ratio		• *If the 2 types (sexes, ages, etc.) of animals do not have the same probability of capture (probable for turkeys), one of the critical assumptions is violated (Krebs 1989:161).* • Designed for situations where one group (sex, age, etc.) is removed more than the other (e.g., spring gobbler hunting) (Krebs 1989).		
Catch-effort		• "This method is highly restricted in its use because it will work only if a large fraction of the population is removed so that there is a decline in the catch per unit effort. It will not work if the population is large relative to the removals" (Krebs 1989:166). • Large samples are usually required (Krebs 1989:166).		
Personal interview-map plot technique (Mosby and Handley 1943, Weaver and Mosby 1979)	• Permits the interviewer the opportunity to assess sportsman attitudes regarding the status and problems of the species in the inventory area (Zirkle 1982, probably paraphrasing Weaver and Mosby 1979 or Mosby and Handley 1943).	• Doesn't census the relatively solitary adult gobblers, which are added to the population estimate by using an approximation formula (Weaver and Mosby 1979).		• One person can cover an entire county in approximately 1 week (Zirkle 1982, probably paraphrasing Weaver and Mosby 1979 or Mosby and Handley 1943).
Double sampling		• If it is assumed that accurate ground counts can be made, then it may be more efficient to take more ground counts and not do any aerial surveying (Eberhardt et al. 1979) (see Cochran 1977:342 for a chart to help make this determination).		

Method	Advantages	Disadvantages	Cost	Manpower
Brood surveys (e.g. total *N* hens and poults seen during routine duties by field officers, or seen by cooperators) (Schultz and McDowell 1957, Wunz and Shope 1980, Wunz and Ross 1990, Lewis 1978, Craig and Suetsugu 1973) May be considered a subheading of roadside counts (Ammann and Ryel 1963).	• *Correlated with fall harvest (Wunz and Shope 1980 in PA, Vangilder unpubl. data, Wunz and Ross 1990).* • *Correlated with the proportion of juvenile gobblers in the subsequent spring's harvest in MO (Kurzejeski and Vangilder 1992).* • Correlated with annual harvest as estimated from a postal survey in PA (Wunz and Ross 1990). • Correlated with hunter report card data in PA (Wunz and Ross 1990). • Can be used to derive poult-to-hen ratios, which are correlated with the proportion of juveniles in the fall harvest and the proportion of juvenile males in the following spring harvest. • *Provide reliable indices to annual reproduction for all subspecies (Kurzejeski and Vangilder 1992)* • Cooperator surveys are relatively inexpensive (compared with gobbling counts) (Backs et al. 1985) • Poult counts provide immediate knowledge of reproduction during the previous year (Smith 1975). • Number of young per hen with brood was shown to provide a reasonable estimate of relative production in Nebraska (Menzel 1975). • Use of cooperators can provide data from a relatively large area (e.g., an entire state). • Are useful to determine the population status prior to the fall, and can be used to develop recommendations for a fall hunting season (Ontario 1985). • Summer brood surveys are more accurate than gobbling counts in spring for determining the fall pre-season population status because of the effects of inclement weather on gobbling (Ontario 1985).	• An index, so lacks the precision of quantitative estimates of density. • No relationship found between poult:hen ratios and subsequent fall harvest in Nebraska (Menzel 1975) (a disadvantage to using brood surveys as a production index, not as an abundance index). • Not correlated with spring harvest data in PA (Wunz and Ross 1990) • Low sample size due to infrequent sightings (Wunz and Shope 1980 as cited in Ontario 1985, Bartush et al. 1985) • Inexperienced surveyors may fail to record sightings (Bartush et al. 1985). • *Lack of standardization (i.e., with respect to same degree of effort each year) may be a problem (Bartush et al. 1985).* • Many variations in the method exist (Ontario 1985). • Broods are often encountered where it is difficult to see the poults (Kimmel and Tzilkowski 1986) (a disadvantage to using brood surveys as a production index, not as an abundance index). • Broods may form multiple-hen broods (Schultz and McDowell 1957) as the summer progresses (Leopold 1944:166) (a disadvantage to using brood surveys as a production index, not as an abundance index). • Biased toward observation associated with public roads and open agricultural areas (Backs et al. 1985). • Brood counts over designated routes were not recommended by Myers (1973) in CO because they are "time consuming and often fruitless." • Broods may be difficult to count because of dense cover, high vegetation, or wariness of the birds (Hoffman 1962) (a disadvantage to using brood surveys as a production index, not as an abundance index). • Underestimates of the broodless hen component of the population are a concern (Lewis and Kurzejeski 1984 as cited in Ontario 1985) (a disadvantage to using brood surveys as a production index, not as an abundance index).	• $450-600/route/year (including expenses and salaries) for 16 annual surveys in FL (Bartush et al. 1985).	• One man-hour per turkey observation (averaging 3 birds/observation) (compared with at least 6-7 man-hours per bird heard for gobbling count surveys), in a study done in Indiana (Backs et al. 1985). • At least 39 samples were needed to reflect yearly changes in brood averages of 10% in CO (Hoffman 1962).

Method	Advantages	Disadvantages	Cost	Manpower
Reports from deer hunters (Welsh and Kimmel 1990, in MN; Lewis 1980, in MO; Garver 1986, in IL; Kimmel et. al. 1996, in MN) **and turkey hunters** (Kennamer 1986).	• *Cost- and labor-effective, compared to route-oriented surveys (Welsh and Kimmel 1990).* • An advantage over landowner-cooperator surveys is that a number of potential survey participants can be easily defined, and data can be collected over a shorter period of time (length of the hunting season) • Distribution of hunters may be relatively even over permit areas, thus making the technique an effective indicator of wild turkey <u>abundance</u> and <u>distribution</u> (Welsh and Kimmel 1990). • Relatively inexpensive. • Requires a minimal amount of labor. • Response rate remains relatively constant (compare with interviewing cooperators, above) (Welsh and Kimmel 1990). • Can detect 10-15% changes in turkeys seen per hunter per day (Welsh and Kimmel 1990). • If hunters are asked for locations of turkey sightings, can also provide useful information on distribution (Kimmel et al. 1996). • **Percent of hunters observing wild turkeys** (HOWT) is more robust to outliers, and better reflects known geographical and annual differences in abundance, than **number of turkeys observed per days hunting** (TPD); hunters may better recollect general sightings than exact numbers seen (Kimmel et al. 1996, with references). • Strongly correlated with subsequent spring harvest (Rolley and Kubisiak 1994, in WI). • Can provide data from a relatively large area (e.g. an entire state). • An index, so lacks the precision	of quantitative estimates of density. • Not possible in areas without hunting seasons (e.g. where turkey populations are not yet well established) • Correlated with the following spring harvest (Welsh and Kimmel 1990, in MN). • Cannot predict actual turkey densities (Welsh and Kimmel 1990) • Percent of hunters observing wild turkeys *(HOWT) is more robust to outliers, and better reflects known geographical and annual differences in abundance,* than **number of turkeys observed per days hunting** (TPD); hunters may better recollect general sightings than exact numbers seen (Kimmel et al. 1996, with references). • An antlerless deer survey	conducted in MN cost $3,500 for 4 mailings (Welsh and Kimmel 1990); this was 63% of the cost of gobble count routes conducted over the same area. • Can be done by 1 individual	in an office . • Can provide data on

Method	Advantages	Disadvantages	Cost	Manpower
Roadside counts/ survey routes (Speake 1980, Beasom 1970, Pattee and Beasom 1979, Shaw 1973, Smith 1962) May be considered to be a tool for gobbling counts.	production, age, and sex, including poult:hen ratios, brood size, and percentage of hens with poults. • Can traverse large areas quickly and easily by using only 2 persons and a vehicle (Brower 1990:120). • "Population sampling is quick, easy, and inexpensive" (Hewitt 1967b, discussing red-winged blackbirds in New York State). • "Counting from a car is particularly good for large and conspicuous birds which occur at low densities, such as raptors" (Bibby et al. 1992:77). • Useful for large regions such as a state. • Useful when access off the existing road system is difficult (Norton-Griffiths 1978:4). • An index, so lacks the precision	of quantitative estimates of density. • More useful in the more open habitats occupied by the Merriam's and Rio Grande subspecies. • Requires an adequate road system. • Turkeys encountered on roads are not visible long enough to make an accurate count (Kimmel and Tzilkowski 1986) • No relation found between average N turkeys seen on established survey routes and hunter harvest in Nebraska (Menzel 1975). • Condition of the roadside cover affects visibility (Davis and Winstead 1980). • Numbers of animals seen are determined by activity of the animals as affected by hour of day, food supply, and weather (Davis and Winstead 1980, Hewitt 1967b) . . . and potentially height and density of vegetation and cloud cover (Sauder et al. 1971). • Activity may vary quantitatively temporally, seasonally, and selectively (Davis and Winstead 1980). • "Although this method provides a reliable index of population changes from year to year or between geographical areas with similar habitats, it is limited for seasonal comparisons because of serious sampling biases caused by changes in food supply and cover" (Brower 1990:121). "The counts obtained from roadside censuses are. . . not comparable. . . from one season to another" (Howell 1951). • Edges of roads tend to be "habitat" for some species (and are avoided by others-SMP), and this leads to a consistent overestimate (underestimate) of numbers or density (Norton-Griffiths 1978:4, Hewitt 1967b). • Roads are rarely distributed randomly across an area...they tend to pass along contours rather than across them (Norton-Griffiths 1978:4). . . road counts are open to considerable bias because the road system is unlikely to be representative of an area. . .more important, the bias is likely to change in the course of the year as the	• A single observer could cover 275 acres per hour, surveying a strip 75 yards on each side of the road (Hewitt 1967b, discussing red-winged blackbirds in New York State).	

II. Indices (continued)

Method	Advantages	Disadvantages	Cost	Manpower
Roadside counts/ survey routes (continued)		distribution of the animals changes (Norton-Griffiths 1978:100). • "There is no straightforward method of calculating the sample error from a road count, for a road system cannot be regarded as a sample of units in the same way as a set of transects" (Norton-Griffiths 1978:102). (But perhaps this is only a problem if roadside counts are to be used as an estimate, rather than an index?) • Good correlation with hunter		
Gobbling counts (Scott and Boeker 1972, Porter and Ludwig 1980, Bevill 1975, Lint et al. 1995)	success rates (Porter and Ludwig 1980, in MN; Palmer et al. 1990, in MS). • Can increase the total number of birds seen or heard compared to a conventional census (see references in Kimmel and Tzilkowski 1986). • Gobbling activity shown to be linked to the hen:gobbler ratio (sex ratio) and "might be useful as population indexes where outside disturbances do not interfere." • *Can be used to monitor range expansion, trends in population growth and the magnitude of differences in population abundance (Porter and Ludwig 1980, in MN).* • May be useful to derive indexes to population levels over time or to compare relative densities between different areas (but not to predict fall harvest) (Stauffer 1993, in a paper about quail). • *Also defines the phenology of gobbling [to determine peak gobbling activity], and that information can then be used to time spring hunting seasons with peak gobbling activity (Porter and Ludwig 1980 as cited in Ontario 1985).* • May be conducted to determine the effect of a severe winter on the breeding population (Ontario 1985). • Doesn't disturb birds as much as more direct estimating methods (Bull 1981). • "Relatively few observers can cover a large area and obtain a large number of observations rather inexpensively even when the density of a species is low" (Bull 1981). • Can sample all types of habitat (Ammann and Ryel 1963). • Quality of data is questionable	(Welsh and Kimmel 1990) and has been claimed to be unreliable as a population indicator (Scott and Boeker 1972). • *Population estimates only weakly correlated with call counts (Palmer et al. 1990)* • *May be related to gobbler condition, such that indices based on call counts may falsely indicate population decline after winters with food shortages (Palmer et al. 1990).* • Gobbling activity appeared to be unrelated to poult production in AZ (Scott and Boeker 1972) • Gobbling varies greatly among individuals and with the chronology of breeding activity, and thus is a limited technique as a population measure (Hoffman 1990, in CO). • Daily variability in gobbling intensity (Wise 1973, Porter 1978). • Gobbling activity may be affected by weather conditions such as cloud cover (Bevill 1973, Davis 1971, as cited in Bevill 1975), dew factor, wind velocity, and rain (Bevill 1973). • Vocalization rates and detectability can be influenced by such factors as wind, rain, time of day, temperature, seasonality, species response traits, lunar cycles, and disturbance by humans or other predators, effects of terrain and vegetation on sound, territoriality, breeding condition (Johnson et al. 1981, Bull 1981) • *Gobbling activity was reduced after winters that had food shortages (Palmer et al. 1990, in MS).* • *WMH: George Hurst's group in Mississippi has found that gobbling is influenced by the*	(Welsh and Kimmel 1990); this was 160% of the cost of an antlerless-deer hunter survey conducted over the same area. • >70 worker-	days by a large number of personnel, in a MN study (see Welsh and Kimmel 1990:132). • Two people for 24 mornings each spring harvest season (Lint et al. 1995). • At least 6-7 man-hours per bird heard (compared with 1 man-hour per turkey observation, averaging 3 birds per observation, for a cooperator survey, in a study done in Indiana (Backs et al. 1985). • Not necessary

Method	Advantages	Disadvantages	Cost	Manpower
Gobbling counts (continued)		*condition of the gobblers—so there is some variation that is not associated with population size.* • Surveys may be hampered by inclement weather (Backs et al. 1985, Donohoe and Martinson 1963). • More expensive and labor intensive compared with techniques such as reports from deer hunters (Welsh and Kimmel 1990), and harvest data (Lint et al. 1995). • Large number of personnel required (Wise 1973) • Requires an adequate road system. • Outside noises may interfere with ability to hear gobbling (Porter and Ludwig 1980 as cited in Ontario 1985). • Difficult to estimate precision (Porter and Ludwig 1980). • Only actively gobbling males are detected (Backs et al. 1985) • Estimates of population size may be dependent on manpower used to survey an area (Donohoe and Martinson 1963). • "In most cases it probably is risky to use call counts to make predictions concerning potential fall harvests, unless such data are supplemented by information on nesting success and survival" (Stauffer 1993, in a paper about quail). • Small sample sizes may be a problem with wild turkeys (Porter and Ludwig 1980 as cited in Ontario 1985). • "Gobbling counts in spring are not as accurate as summer brood surveys for determining the fall pre-season population status because of the effects of inclement weather on gobbling" (Ontario 1985). • Shifting personnel may differ in hearing ability and so produce records that may not be comparable (Ammann and Ryel 1963). • Methods used to monitor and quantify gobbling have differed among studies, making comparisons difficult (Hoffman 1990). • $5,600 for a study in MN		

Method	Advantages	Disadvantages	Cost	Manpower
Snow-track counts (track counts) May be considered a subset of direct winter counts.	to observe birds directly • Can provide sex information (Burke 1982 as cited in Ontario 1985). Winter sex ratio functions as an index of the potential breeding population, and may also provide a post-season estimate of the number of gobblers versus hens harvested (Wooley et al. 1978 as cited in Ontario 1985). • The resulting winter sex ratios provide a post-season estimate of the number of gobblers vs. hens harvested (Wooley et al. 1978 as cited in Ontario 1985). The counts then also function as an index of the potential breeding population (Ontario 1985). • Tracks are easily found • Birds are easy to observe because of lack of cover in the winter (Hurt 1968 as cited in Ontario 1985). • Easily and inexpensively conducted (Wooley et al. 1978 as cited in Ontario 1985). • *Can be used to find and map flock locations during periods of good snow cover.* • In some areas (e.g. Indiana, Wise	1973), a large percentage of turkeys do not appear to move appreciably during periods of temporary snow cover. • *Data collection may be interrupted by inclement weather (Hayden and Wunz 1975 as cited in Ontario 1985). WMH: The biggest problem is getting suitable tracking conditions; depends on consistent and persistent snow cover.* • Toms and hens behave differently in the winter where hens are often found in large aggregates (Ontario 1985) • Small sample size, especially in populations not yet established (Wooley et al. 1978 as cited in Ontario 1985). • Tracks are remote from the animal in time; and it is difficult to determine how many birds made the tracks (Bull 1981). • "Caution must be exercised in using these data, as one animal may cross a transect or plot several times. Therefore, these counts should be considered an index of activity rather than a measure of abundance" (Brower 1990:122).		
Nuisance/ damage complaints		• *Harvest/unit effort and*		
Harvest data (may be standardized using hunter effort), e.g., postal surveys, bag checks.	*number of harvested gobblers has been shown to be related to mark-recapture population estimates (Lint et al. 1995).* • *May indicate trends better than population estimates (Bailey 1980).* • Many wildlife management areas may already be collecting data needed for the harvested-gobblers index; *managers can compile <u>existing</u> hunter effort information to examine possible trends and relations between harvested gobblers and hunter effort for their gobbler population (Lint et al. 1995)* • *Harvest data are relatively easy and inexpensive to collect (Lint et al. 1995, Stauffer 1993).* • Direct biological data, such as weight, age, and sex, may be collected from harvested birds at check stations. • Bias in sex and age ratios (Wunz	and Shope 1980). • After-the-fact information may have little use in planning future hunting seasons (Wunz and Shope 1980). • Harvest/unit effort not as useful an index when harvest greatly influences population size (Lint et al. 1995). • Operation of a check station is time consuming. • *The proportion of the total population that is harvested (harvest rate) must be constant for areas or time periods being compared (Lancia et al. 1994:223). WMH: Fall, either-sex harvest data are difficult to interpret because (a) food availability affects harvest, (b) concurrent seasons for other species also affect harvest (harvest rate may remain constant as population declines because turkeys are taken by hunters pursuing other species).* • Hunter report cards provide	survey at 1985 postage rates cost $70,450 (Kurzejeski and Vangilder 1992), plus data entry and analysis costs; a fall survey cost an additional $35,000 plus data entry and analysis costs. • In Missouri, the costs for spring and fall mandatory check stations average $40,000 annually (Kurzejeski and Vangilder 1992). • Can estimate	

Method	Advantages	Disadvantages	Cost	Manpower
Harvest data (continued)		less accurate data than check stations (Myers 1973). • Hunter surveys may provide an insufficient sample size to provide regional or county information (Kurzejeski and Vangilder 1992). • Results may not be available in time for the regulation setting of the next year's hunting season or for making available to the public in a timely fashion (Kurzejeski and Vangilder 1992). • Hunters may have forgotten pertinent information by the time surveys reach them (Kurzejeski and Vangilder 1992). • The data source may be of variable reliability (hunters) and there is a lack of control over data quality (lack of variance estimates, etc.). The data may not lend itself to statistical analyses, and thus it is difficult to identify real differences between areas or years. At best, we are limited to general statements about population trends from hunter data (Stauffer 1993). • Hunters tend to inflate their reported hunting success through pride, prestige, or memory loss, causing large biases. Those hunters who bag nothing are the worst offenders (Seber 1982:489). • Successful hunters tend to respond at a higher rate than unsuccessful hunters (Kurzejeski and Vangilder 1992). • Hunter surveys do not allow the collection of some biological data that may be collected at check stations (Kurzejeski and Vangilder 1992). • Obtaining mailing lists and recovering mail surveys takes a lot of time—may be up to a year and a half after the end of the season before the data are available (Kurzejeski and Vangilder 1992). • In Missouri, a spring mail		

Method	Advantages	Disadvantages	Cost	Manpower
Feeding sites (scratch marks, pellets, etc.)				
Dusting sites		• "Because dusting regulates the amount of lipid substance on the feathers,... the amount of dusting may be in response to environmental factors (e.g., diet), so caution should be used in comparisons between populations" (Bull 1981).		
Dropping/fecal/ pellet counts	the relative numbers of individuals, demonstrate population fluctuations, and also determine preferred habitat types and seasonal use patterns (Neff 1968 as cited in Ontario 1985). • Dropping configuration is useful in revealing the sex of the birds (Bailey 1956 as cited in Ontario 1985). • "Some of the problems associated with counting actual populations do not occur when counting droppings" [the author does not elaborate] (Ontario 1985).	• Observer fatigue, boredom, and lack of experience contribute to missed groups [and therefore cause bias] (Ontario 1985). • The possibility of counting the same droppings from a previous year is a source of error (Ontario 1985). • Durability of scat and resistance to weather, diet, behavior, and time must be considered (Bull 1981). • Loss of dropping groups by erosion and insect attack increase variations between years as do defecation rates where an increase in dropping density may be due to an ample food supply in a particular year, not an increase in population (Ontario 1985).		
Frequency indices	• Useful when it is difficult to count the number of individuals in a unit, but easy to determine the presence or absence of individuals. • SMP: Useful for measuring distribution.			
Poult survival studies, based on radiotelemetry	• High poult mortality was shown to be the major factor controlling population density in AL (Everett et al. 1980).	• May not be an accurate indicator of overall productive success when only a small percentage (<40%) of the hens are radio-tagged (Everett et al. 1980).		

IV. Tools for the above techniques

Method	Advantages	Disadvantages	Cost	Manpower
Radiotelemetry	• Advantage over mark-recapture as a separate technique: often provides insight into sources of mortality (and sometimes even estimates of source-specific mortality risks) and information about emigration (Pollock et al. 1990:67). • When used for mark-recapture studies, resightings are generally much cheaper to acquire than physically capturing and handling the animals (White 1996). • Allows determination of the location and status of individuals without having to flush or disturb the birds (Stauffer 1993). • Could increase the effectiveness of using tape-recorded calls to lure hens for brood counts (Tefft 1996a,b).	Relatively expensive, in both equipment costs and the substantial field effort needed to obtain frequent locations on a large number of animals (Pollock et al. 1990:67). • There may sometimes be a lack of independence between losses of contact and animal status, and such a dependence could cause problems in estimation (Pollock et al. 1990:67). • When used for mark-recapture, unmarked animals are not marked on subsequent occasions (White 1996).		
Summer baiting (2 indices described by Hayden 1985) May be used as a tool for brood surveys, or for capturing birds for use in mark-recapture estimates.	• Makes visible turkeys that might otherwise never be seen (Hayden 1985); quickly attracts birds to roads where they can be counted (Ontario 1985). • Bait station routes can be easily established. • Personnel can be trained quickly to bait and examine stations .	• Resulting fall population estimates need to be adjusted depending on mast production (Hayden 1985). • Turkeys may not find the bait attractive if a natural food supply is plentiful (Ontario 1985).		
Winter baiting May be used as a tool for capturing birds for use in mark-recapture estimates.	• Counts appeared to be reliable in CO (Myers 1973). • Recommended technique to concentrate birds for census in CO (Myers 1973). • Provide "as accurate an indicator of population trends as is possible to obtain" (Myers 1973). • Turkey counts can be tallied by counting tracks in fresh snow (need not see birds themselves) (Myers 1973).	The majority (25 of 31) feed stations were not found by turkeys in CO (Myers 1973) .		
Mail-carrier surveys (a tool for roadside counts/brood surveys)	• The daily routines of the participants are consistent (Ammann and Ryel 1963). • The counts can be taken whenever the information is needed the most, or when the habits of the birds are most likely to yield consistent results (Ammann and Ryel 1963). • Helps acquaint the carriers (many of whom are hunters) with the management program (Ammann and Ryel 1963).			

Method	Advantages	Disadvantages	Cost	Manpower
Camera stations May be used as a tool for brood surveys.				
Adaptive sampling	• Sampling intensity used in a given area depends on the density found in the previous area(s), with sampling then concentrated in the higher-density areas; useful if the population is very patchy and the population area is very large (Seber 1986).			
Stratification A statistical tool for various sampling techniques.	• "As populations tend to be very patchy, stratified sampling seems to be the most appropriate method" (Seber 1986). • WMH: Many states are already stratified along management zones.			
Infrared sensing imagery	• Can greatly increase detection rates over standard aerial survey techniques (Naugle et al. 1996). • High cost may be justifiable in areas where current methods of estimating density are questionable (Naugle et al. 1996).	• Untrained interpreters may lack the ability to distinguish false targets (see Naugle et al. 1996 with references) and usually count more individuals than skilled interpreters (see Naugle et al. 1996 with references). • Overlapping transects may cause biases (Naugle et al. 1996 discuss ways to correct for these). • Higher cost than visual aerial transect sampling (Naugle et al. 1996). • May not be cost-effective in open habitats where less expensive techniques (e.g., visual aerial counts) reliably estimate density (Naugle et al. 1996).	\$99 per km^2 scanned (including cost of flying to study area, per diem for 2 people, and analysis of infrared tapes), for a deer survey in South Dakota in 1994 (Naugle et al. (1996).	
Tape-recorded calls **(poult distress calls, male vocalizations)** (Kimmel and Tzilkowski 1986)	• Cost and time/labor effective (Johnson et al. 1981). • *Useful for luring broods into open areas where visibility of poults would be optimum (Kimmel and Tzilkowski 1986).* • *Can be used "to elicit a vocal or visual response from an otherwise silent or invisible animal"* (Norton-Griffiths 1978:107). • Can increase sample size by eliciting responses from birds that are elusive and not easy to detect visually (Marion et al. 1981, Johnson et al. 1981).	• An index, so lacks the precision of quantitative estimates of density. • Males do not respond to taped call. • An important source of bias is the failure of a certain proportion of the population to respond to auditory signals (Marion et al. 1981, Johnson et al. 1981). • For some bird species, "indiscriminate use of playback recordings on repeated visits during the breeding season can bias the results as birds may alter their habits or their terrestrial		

Method	Advantages	Disadvantages	Cost	Manpower
Tape-recorded calls (poult distress calls, male vocalizations) (continued)	• A playback recording census can increase the total number of birds seen or heard for a given species in comparison to a conventional census, especially for species with low song activity (Johnson et al. 1981). • Some species of birds may respond to tape recordings at times when they would otherwise remain silent (Johnson et al. 1981, with references). • In a study of blue grouse, hooting males were counted faster and a total census was obtained sooner by eliciting the response of males to the recorded calls of a hen (Stirling and Bendell 1966).	boundaries if they believe a competing member of the same species is holding territory nearby" (Johnson et al. 1981). • "If censused too often some individuals and/or species may become less responsive" (Johnson et al. 1981). • Response rates and detectability can be influenced by such factors as wind, rain, time of day, temperature, seasonality, species response traits, lunar cycles, and disturbance by humans or other predators, effects of terrain and vegetation on sound, territoriality, breeding condition (Johnson et al. 1981, Bull 1981, Stirling and Bendell 1966-possible effects of wind and other weather on blue grouse). • Proved ineffective at locating turkey broods in Rhode Island (Tefft 1996a,b), but could be improved with the aid a radio transmitters.		

The end of a successful spring gobbler hunt, E. S. "Sam" Nenno, Monongalia County, West Virginia, 1982.
U.S. Forest Service, E.S. Nenno.

U.S. Department of the Interior
U.S. Fish & Wildlife Service
Route 1, Box 166
Sheperdstown, WV 25443

http://www.fws.gov/

April 2000